MINDING THE
EDGE

MINDING THE
EDGE

STRATEGIES FOR A FULFILLING,
SUCCESSFUL CAREER AS AN ACTOR

CARL MENNINGER AND LORI HAMMEL

WAVELAND

PRESS, INC.

Long Grove, Illinois

For information about this book, contact:
   Waveland Press, Inc.
   4180 IL Route 83, Suite 101
   Long Grove, IL 60047-9580
   (847) 634-0081
   info@waveland.com
   www.waveland.com

Cover design by Blue House

10-digit ISBN 1-57766-711-5
13-digit ISBN 978-1-57766-711-7

Printed in the United States of America

7   6   5   4   3   2

Contents

Preface

A PREFACE FROM CARL (The Professor)

Several years ago, Lori was a guest speaker in my Audition Techniques class at American University. She shared her experience as an actor and gave tips to the students. Before the class, we met and discussed her outline for the two-and-a-half-hour session. I was impressed that her workshop combined practical experience and a positive mental approach to "the business." I told her that she should write a book. She laughed and responded that she wouldn't know where to start. Thus began our collaboration on this project—one in a long line of many collaborations.

In this book, we marry the perspectives of both actor and educator. Lori is continually amazed that young actors are not taught how to cope with "the business," how to create a plan, and how to manage their careers. Framing the wisdom and insights derived from her successful acting career into a format and language that speaks to college actors was my job as coauthor. The book is designed as a supplement for an acting class or an audition class. Most actor-training programs offer semester-long courses in audition techniques for the working actor. There are many wonderful books that address auditioning, marketing, agents, resumes, cover letters, etc. *Minding the Edge* (MTE) is the precursor to those texts. This book provides a framework in which to place the practical advice that those other publications offer.

A PREFACE FROM LORI (The Actor)

My sincere hope is that this book will raise important personal and professional questions. It is meant to give you a realistic, hopeful perspective about "the business" and illuminate strategies that can lead to success. Once you have integrated those strategies, pass along what you have learned to others on the same path. Sharing your philosophy and perspectives will not only solidify and strengthen your beliefs, it will also force you to "walk the talk."

HOW INSTRUCTORS CAN USE THIS BOOK

Instructors can ask students to do the exercises we've devised. Some were designed as in-class exercises and others were meant for students to complete on their own. We hope the exercises generate discussion, and to that end, we've interspersed discussion questions throughout the text that may jump-start the process. The same questions can also serve as prompts for journal or notebook entries.

However the book is used, the intention is to prepare young actors for the challenges "the business" presents. We hope you'll find the kind of positive energy in reading and utilizing it that we found in writing it.

ACKNOWLEDGEMENTS

We need to thank the following people for their feedback, support, and faith in us, especially Cara Gabriel and Gary Dontzig who gave us invaluable feedback that dramatically changed the rewrite process. Michael Baron, Ruth Bender, Barry Brown, Jennifer Cumberworth, Saidah Ekulon, Jessica Feirtag, Gary Garrison, Ryan Graham, Pamela and James Hammel, Stacey Harris, Steven Hauck, Jeanie Hopkins, Dr. Diana Kirschner, Karl Kippola, Matthew Knauer, Matt Lenz, Adrian Martinez, Michael Mastro, Neal Mayer, Catherine Menninger, Ed Menninger, Karen Murphy, Jeni Ogilvie, Harry Palmer, Matthew Prescott, Daniel Rakowski, Mark Ramont, Tania Richard, Javier

Rivera, Nicholas Rodriguez, Alec Satin, Amanda Scheirer, Chris Schriever, Mike Schwartz, Matt Shea, Todd Sherry, Nyk Schmalz, Margo Seibert, Bill Selby, Caleen Sinnette-Jennings, Albert and Mary Jane Slepyan, Carolyn Tucci, Stephen Wallem, Debra Wanger-Yaruss, Bill Yule, Kristine Zbornik, and finally, Thomas Curtin for believing in the importance of this book and its message.

Introduction

Minding the Edge uses two informed points of view to provide you with a perspective that takes into account both your current place in the professional journey as well as the realities of life as a working actor. Throughout the book you'll read Lori's *Dispatches from the Field* and Carl's *Dispatches from the Field*. These "notes" allow us to share our individual experiences and the lessons they've taught us. You might identify with some of the examples Carl uses because you may have experienced or are experiencing some of the situations he describes. Lori's stories enable you to see that actors need to constantly reassess and develop new goals and strategies as the industry changes. We hope our insights help illuminate your path to fulfillment and success.

In addition to our perspectives, strategies, and stories, you will read many quotes throughout the book. You may not recognize the names of the people quoted. Some are actors, others are playwrights, directors, and producers, but all of them have forged successful, fulfilling careers in "the business." We think their insights and wisdom are valuable and worthwhile. You don't have to be a famous superstar to have a satisfying, successful career.

We'd like to start with some important questions. This is the first of many exercises designed to help define and take stock of your *current* place and mind-set, as well as raise important questions that you'll need to answer as you approach "the business." Treat this book like a journal. We left space after each question to write your answers, and there are blank pages at the end of the book to write longer answers.

Assessment Questions

Exercise: **Please answer the following questions as honestly as possible. The answers are for your eyes only. Set aside about 45 minutes to do this.**

When do you graduate?

What feelings arise when you envision life after graduation?

How will you find work as an actor the day after you graduate?

What are your goals as an actor? How do you define personal success?

How many of those goals have you achieved?

Where will you live to pursue your acting career?

Why did you choose that city?

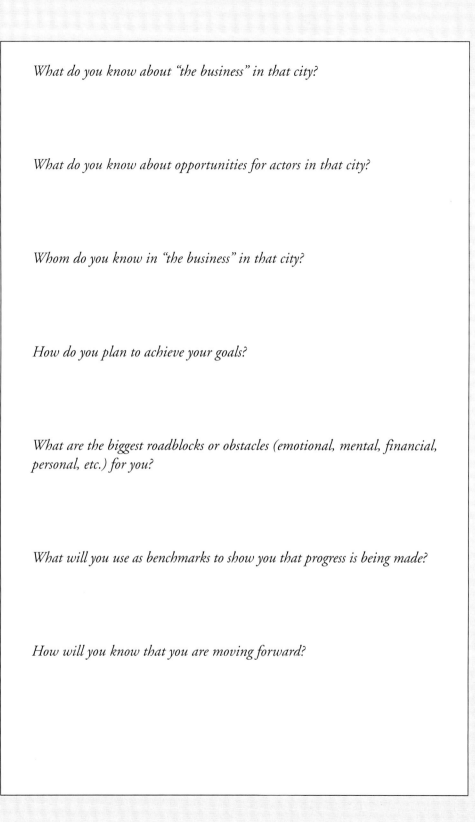

What do you know about "the business" in that city?

What do you know about opportunities for actors in that city?

Whom do you know in "the business" in that city?

How do you plan to achieve your goals?

What are the biggest roadblocks or obstacles (emotional, mental, financial, personal, etc.) for you?

What will you use as benchmarks to show you that progress is being made?

How will you know that you are moving forward?

How will you know when you're successful? What are your measures of success?

What have been your sources of motivation in the past?

How do you deal with setbacks or disappointment?

How do you deal with your feelings when a show closes?

Who do you have on your support team now?

How do they help you overcome obstacles, setbacks, and fears?

Can you do any of that for yourself?

Now take a moment to think about your reaction to the questionnaire.

What questions never occurred to you before? Why?

How did the questions change or alter your perspective as far as entering the professional world?

This questionnaire should serve as a reality check. Are there questions you couldn't answer? If so, don't panic. *Minding the Edge* will help you clarify what you already know and help you identify what you don't, so that you can make informed decisions as you advance in your career.

By the time you finish this book, we hope that you will have made important personal and professional discoveries. Consider taking this questionnaire again after you've read *Minding the Edge*. You may be surprised to find that your answers reflect a deeper understanding of your current situation, goals, challenges, and resources.

Chapter 1

A Different Kind of "How To"

Mind-Set Makes the Difference

Creating a meaningful life and career starts with your mind-set: a point of view that serves as a filter and an internal support system for your business and personal life. How you view yourself and your work informs all of your successes and relationships. A constructive mind-set, combined with talent, skills, and business knowledge, is a powerful way to engage with the world. Choosing to live in that mind-set and implement strategies that grow from it can lead to a successful, fulfilling career. Think of this book as a manual, a step-by-step guide to a useful and perhaps new mind-set.

There are few courses that address the specific mind-set this business requires. While you can easily find courses that instruct young actors in audition techniques, or senior showcases that expose students to agents and casting directors, these courses don't address an overall strategy for success. Young actors are seldom required to think about themselves and their interactions in the "real world." They may find tremendous success and fulfillment in a college or training environment, but managing the realities of a professional career (that goes beyond work onstage or on camera) poses a significant challenge.

By fulfillment, we mean the feeling of professional satisfaction and contentment that are the reward for one's hard work, creativity, passion, and artistic endeavors. If you experience these, you will find that your career will be satisfying, enriching, and most likely successful. Fulfillment comes with success.

Think of this book as a manual, a step-by-step guide to a useful and perhaps new mind-set.

How many times have you been asked, "What will you do when you're done with school?" You may have answered something like this, "I'm moving to (fill in name of city here) to be an actor." While this is certainly a fine answer, it's not a game plan. Your career doesn't begin the day you leave school. It begins while you're still studying. Now is the time to create a plan and equip yourself with the tools to implement all that you've learned in your acting training. The time to grab the bull by the horns and start taking control of your career is now. It's too challenging an industry to begin figuring out after you leave school. Don't wait until you're on stage at graduation to start the process.

In working with young actors on the university and professional level, we see a gap. Before actors graduate and enter "the business," they need to:

- possess a specific understanding of managing and sustaining their acting careers and utilize that understanding to devise strategies for success.
- cultivate a mind-set that will lead to a successful and satisfying career.
- learn to see the industry with a specific, constructive point of view and use that perspective to design strategies to achieve their goals.

We wrote this book because when you graduate from college or first enter "the business" you'll be "thrown in the pool" and expected to either sink or swim. The same thing happened to us. We wanted to save you much of the trial and error we experienced (not that you won't experience plenty) and share our perspectives on creating a fulfilling career. In this book, we pinpoint the qualities and explain habits that will help you achieve success as an actor.

Our goal is simple:

To inspire, empower, and educate young actors to create a positive mind-set and disciplined habits, actions, and ways of thinking that will shape their vision of success and lead to fulfillment in the entertainment industry.

Try to think of your career as one in which success and fulfillment are interconnected. You can have career success and not experience fulfillment, but success is firmly planted within the notion of fulfillment. Why else would you feel fulfilled? So, you may want to alter your definition of success by factoring in fulfillment.

Success is firmly planted within the notion of fulfillment.

Most people's first experience with the traditional pattern of work is as a student. Sometime around age six we arrive at school, and the teacher presents a curriculum that is developmentally and sequentially appropriate. The paradigm goes like this: teacher explains concept, teacher gives students work so they can implement concept, students complete work, teacher assesses. The students master the concepts (success is determined by the level of mastery) and move on to the next grade level and teacher. And so it goes, until we graduate from college.

When people get to the "real world," the same paradigm applies: Boss gives employee a task. Employee performs task. Success is measured by how well employee performs the task. Employee is rewarded with more money, more vacation, more responsibility, bigger office—you get the idea. As an actor, however, you won't work in this paradigm. There won't be anyone assigning you the tasks or telling you how to develop a business plan or how to find work. You are on your own. Even if you are lucky enough to get an agent immediately after graduation, that agent will not find you all of your work. There is not one specific path to a successful career as an actor. Being talented isn't enough. You will have to create the path, and you'll need to create one that allows you to define success and fulfillment on your own terms.

Actors are trained to connect on stage, to analyze, to risk, and to find the through-line. Actors are trained to explore and utilize the collaborative process. They train their voices and bodies. They learn to think like artists and creative beings, but in the end, actors are set loose in the world and told to figure out the business of "the business." And if they have the smarts, they do, and discover success as creative artists.

We ask you to look at "the business" and yourself from a variety of vantage points. This book is a template for creating a positive mind-set as well as setting and achieving attainable goals. While we assume that our target audience is the actor at the beginning of his or her career, this book is useful to any artist at any point in his or her career. It will help you lay a foundation for the way you want to exist, function, experience, and interact in the industry.

This book is a template for creating a positive mind-set as well as setting and achieving attainable goals.

We ask that you commit to the exercises and the reflections in this book because the concepts we present need to be anchored within you and incorporated into your daily life. The exercises will put these concepts into practice and set you on a journey that will lead to useful daily habits. These habits will provide internal stability in a profession that is both unpredictable and volatile. We hope these habits will contribute directly to your success and happiness not only as a professional but also as a human being.

We're not saying that once you adopt these tools, fulfillment will come instantly or without effort. Changing your operating system is not easy. There is an old Zen parable: *What do you do before enlightenment? Chop wood, carry water. What do you do after enlightenment? Chop wood, carry water.* Even after challenging and shifting your outlook and habits, you'll still need to "chop and carry," but you'll have a clearer mind-set and a new set of tools with which to do all that chopping and carrying. Changing your way of thinking doesn't mean that managing a career and your happiness will be less work, but we believe it will be more focused, deliberate, and empowering.

Dispatches from the Field—Carl

Recently, I sat at a cattle call audition for the League of Washington Theatres. More than 60 local theatres joined together for an annual open call for their upcoming seasons. The actors were given 90 seconds to do anything they wished—perform a monologue, sing, juggle—you name it. These auditions lasted four days for about seven hours a day—a mind-numbing experience for the auditors.

As I watched the parade of actors, most of whom did a respectable job, it occurred to me that many of them would leave "the business" because they couldn't "hack it." Every actor has heard the sage advice—don't be an actor unless you can't envision yourself doing anything else. I wonder how many of those actors had asked themselves the questions you answered in the Introduction before they graduated?

OKAY, SO WHAT'S "MINDING THE EDGE"?

Think about the word "edge." *Edge* has both negative and positive connotations. In this book, we will ask you to think about *edge* in multiple ways.

"Don't get close to the edge!" Certainly that's a common phrase for tourists visiting the Grand Canyon. The edge can be the drop-off point. And unless you're minding the edge, you can launch yourself into a free fall. Actors need to be up-to-date with the shifting nature of the industry and its constant changes and trends. Many people are lulled into a false sense of security without putting thought into and keeping track of their vision of fulfillment and career goals. Some actors fall into the trap of thinking that because they have an acting job, they don't need to keep the ball rolling by looking for the next one.

In more traditional career paths, the "edges" aren't as evident since most job seekers view employment with a long-range focus, assuming that the new position will provide some security and that they won't have to look for another job any time soon. The newly employed person envisions a job that will last longer than six weeks or even six months. Most people imagine they will remain with a company for years.

In the entertainment industry, the "edge" is always in sight since gigs are generally short-lived, and it's expected that a project will operate within a limited time frame. An actor's career is made up of a succession of jobs. Shows close, movies wrap, and TV series come to an end. There are famous actors in Hollywood who finish work on a film and panic that there won't be another one. "I'll never work again!" That mentality and anxiety parallels the college senior who faces graduation with trepidation and the fear-based internal monologue "I'll never work!" This volatility requires an actor to embrace a freelance mentality, since the "edge" (or perhaps the abyss) of a job ending is considered the status quo.

> The most crucial element of success for me is to never stop learning. Even in the worst situations, including the projects you want to run screaming from, there is always something to be learned. Take classes, coach, take lessons, watch theatre, listen to music . . . never stop growing.
> — Nicholas Rodriguez, actor

Minding the Edge is all about strengthening the necessary skills that build bridges from one "edge" to the next experience. It's expected that actors be fully committed to studying and improving their craft. This is basically respecting the "show" of "show business," but what about the other half—the "business"? It's imperative to begin simultaneously practicing ways to set up your "business" as an actor, and the best time to start applying these skills is now. By MTE and doing the exercises in this book, you will begin to engage in the planning and practical applications of running your business as an actor. Don't wait until you are handed your diploma. Integrating these business strategies will help you take the "edge" off your anxiety because your actions will be moving you forward.

Dispatches from the Field—Lori

Early in my career, I was an actor who pretended as though the temporary lifestyle on the road or out of town would last forever. I didn't prepare for the future (as in, the day I came off the road). It's hard for me to admit, but I really wasn't minding my edge. I spent money as fast as I made it, and I didn't let people in "the business" know when I would be back to town. This made it doubly hard when I made the leap from the fantasyland called employment back to the reality of finding my next job. I didn't see that I needed to provide myself with a financial cushion once the job ended—a cushion that would help me through the time of uncertainty before the next job. Why did I operate this way? Well, I didn't see the bigger picture, and I didn't know how to be a successful businessperson who is also an actor. I felt as though it was dumb luck that I got hired at all.

Eventually, I changed the way I ran my business as an actor. I began to see the strategies that weren't working and took the necessary steps toward valuing myself as a person who deserved stability. Why did I change? I guess I was tired of being broke and playing the role of valiant, bohemian, "starving artist."

Years later, when I was out of town working with a terrific bunch of actors, I was struck by how many people did what I had done—live the fantasy lifestyle while on the road. By that time, I had chosen to save money while I earned that good salary. My savings enabled me to finance some of my own projects—projects such as my one-woman shows.

I also learned that in order to maintain continuity with my professional relationships in New York, I had to stay in touch with agents and business contacts while I was on the road and let them know, in advance, when I was due back in town. This communication enabled them to help me transition from being in a national tour of a Broadway musical to life back in New York without a job. While on the road, I also put together game plans that would improve my professional life once the show closed.

Eventually, I learned to make my transitions, my re-entry process, more graceful. Even though actors create magical characters and wonderful worlds for others to enjoy, we really have to learn to create wonderful worlds for ourselves as well. It is always important to mind your edges and maintain professional relationships—even when you're out of town.

"I've got to maintain my edge." In this instance, we mean a more positive connotation for the word. Here, your edge is what keeps you on top of your game. It's what keeps you vital. The idea of maintaining your edge means that you are constantly aware, constantly evaluating, and constantly moving forward toward your desired goal. Not only is it about running your "business," but it also means taking classes, keeping your instrument in top form, and maintaining an awareness of the industry. Defining and managing the way the world sees you and the way you see yourself, rather than relinquishing that definition to others, is a critical piece of minding the edge. It's about being ready for the next opportunity rather than losing faith in your abilities and focusing on your setbacks. When you are proactive in this way, you operate from a position of strength and power. You control what you can control and take charge of your career. Without being aware, many actors slowly drift away from MTE. They find excuses, are lulled into complacency, and lose sight of the fact that they are responsible for looking out for their best interests. Here's an example.

Dispatches from the Field—Carl

One of my students, a talented young actor, moved to New York and found a wonderful temp job. She was free to come and go and create her own schedule. Because she was bright, talented, and organized, her value to the company quickly increased. They offered her more money, benefits, and more responsibility. She, in turn, became comfortable with the stability and the financial reward that this job provided. The routine and the camaraderie associated with being part of a group of workers were satisfying. Soon, she found that there was no time for auditions, making contacts, networking, and working toward her acting goals. This certainly would have been fine if she had embraced her new career choice, but that was not the case. On the one hand, she complained about missing her creative life, and on the other she made excuses for all the reasons she couldn't get to classes, go to auditions, or devote the kind of time and energy needed to be an actor. She wondered what happened to the career she had envisioned. Clearly, she lost her edge and lost sight of her own goals and fulfillment.

"He has a real edge to him." "Why are you so edgy?" Obviously, we don't want people thinking of us this way. Nor do we enjoy dealing with people who have a nasty, acerbic edge. They can be unpredictable, disrespectful, difficult, demanding, sarcastic, cynical, temperamental, and negative. (If you've exhibited any of these behaviors lately, it's time to mind this edge.) You need to watch your thinking and behavior so that you don't become one of the "edgy" people.

Learning to create strategies that keep you from becoming that actor with a negative "edge" is critical to your success and longevity in the industry. Young actors need to develop mechanisms that keep negative people from disturbing their equilibrium and adversely influencing their journey. You will also need to deal effectively and professionally with them when you can't avoid them.

Think about these questions: Have you worked with someone who makes others uncomfortable? Someone whose needs and demands seem unreasonable? How about those who are withholding, selfish, or judgmental? Have you ever watched someone treat subordinates disrespectfully? How do you feel when you watch someone refuse to be a team player? Do you enjoy being around a person who diminishes your accomplishments and successes? Remember, if someone talks negatively about others, it might not be hard to imagine that he or she could be talking negatively about you as well.

PUTTING IT INTO ACTION

When you are minding the edge you are in control of what you can control. You manage your vision and definition of success as well as your actions and interactions. You consistently mind the edge through assessing your career choices, both large and small. You have a choice as to how you will run your business and interact with the profession. As you advance in your career, you redefine your goals and definitions of professional satisfaction.

Just like the circus performers who spin multiple plates on long thin dowels, you must constantly be aware of the many edges that need ongoing attention. You must keep all the plates balanced and spinning or they will crash to the ground. It is a nonstop process and a rewarding one when you experience the success you seek.

WHY START MINDING THE EDGE NOW?

Stay open to the ideas in this book. They will add to the arsenal of information that will lead to your success. We may ask you to examine concepts and notions you haven't considered that can help define your values and determine your next actions.

It's our assumption that you're in the early stage of your career. Hopefully, the world hasn't made you jaded or cynical. (If it has, isn't now a better time to shift your mind-set rather than suffering through years of the alternative?) Therefore, we believe you still possess the optimistic energy that has driven you to this point.

Adopt the concepts in this book, skip the jaded and cynical route, and create a professionally fulfilling pathway. Now is the best time to embark on this journey. It is easier to create a habit at the beginning of your journey rather than undoing self-sabotaging and nasty-edge habits later. Minding the edge will help you stay ahead of the game.

Implementing these concepts will make you a smarter and more informed actor because you will have examined your motivations and reasons for being on this challenging journey. Notice that we didn't name this book "How to Become a Superstar." (Although that doesn't mean that implementing these concepts *won't* help you become a "superstar," if it is your desire and path.)

How extraordinary it would be for you to experience both visibility and respect in the industry as a fulfilled, grounded, and generous actor. If you want to find out how acclaimed actors became who they are today, read their biographies, do research and study their trajectories to success. Learn your lessons from their success stories and heed their advice. Remember, they had journeys that got them where they are—success didn't just happen.

HERE'S HOW WE'LL GO ABOUT IT

In order for this book to make sense and be effective, you will need to invest time doing the exercises. You may be tempted to read the book and only imagine the experience of doing the exercises, but in the end, you will miss your personal discoveries. We began by saying this is a *how to* book. In order for any of this to be worthwhile you'll need to do the "what" that leads you to the "how."

It is one thing to read about a concept or a behavior—it is an entirely different experience to implement that concept, engage in it in a meaningful way, and incorporate it into your life. This process is designed to awaken your potential, get you excited about your possibilities, and enable you to feel power and ownership of your career. So, in order to get there, we'll ask you to perform various exercises, journal entries, and observations. As with the questions in the Introduction, we've left space so you can write your entries in this book. There are also blank pages at the end of the book. You may want to keep a journal or a "minding the edge" file on your computer. By expressing your thoughts in writing you will force yourself to articulate your ideas and examine your thinking.

REASONS NOT TO DO THE EXERCISES

While we are optimists, we also are realists. We know that some actors will read this book and decide not to participate in the process. They will look at the activities and exercises and think, "those sound interesting," but they will not take the time to do them.

Rather than finding excuses for not doing the work, we'll make it easy on you by providing the excuses for you. Choose any and all that fit.

- I want to read it through and see what the book is like. I'll read it again. (Translation: Fat chance.)

- I can get the point from reading it. I am good at that. I can visualize myself doing the exercises. (Translation: I am too lazy.)

- My mind-set and outlook are already positive, thank you very much. (Translation: I copped out.)

- By reading the exercises I have a clear understanding of what Lori and Carl are communicating. The exercises are really a waste of my valuable time. (Translation: I don't really want to examine my thoughts and actions.)

- I feel foolish doing these activities. They seem juvenile and silly. (Translation: I'm too cool for this.)

- I am pleased with my professional satisfaction. I just thought this book might be useful for some friends of mine. (Translation: I am deluding myself.)

- I am only reading this book because it's required reading for my class. (Translation: I am only reading this book because it's required for a class.)

The exercises are avenues for personal discovery. If you don't do the exercises and activities you can still be successful, fulfilled, and live a fruitful life. We don't suggest that this is the miracle panacea. However, we do believe that the concepts in this book might make the journey easier.

Chapter 2

You the Actor . . . You the Person

Defining Motivation and Fulfillment

If you have the soul of an artist, be in the world. Have healthy and satisfying relationships. Surround yourself with people who may not be artists but who also do amazing things in the world. If you have the soul of an artist, nobody can take that away from you—whether you're working a job-job to pay the rent, or you're at home raising a family. There's no such thing as a detour, all roads lead to your art. Love your life, love yourself, love others around you and find the good in whatever job you're doing. All that will make you a richer, more productive human being. If you have the soul of an artist, you will find a way to do your art. Make it stunningly beautiful and deeply satisfying, even when, and especially, if you're the only one in the audience.

— Caleen Sinnette Jennings, playwright

Now it's time to get to the nitty-gritty. This section of the book offers you a way to reflect on the person you are, identify the motivation behind your desire for success, define professional fulfillment, and articulate your long-term goals. While you might think you have already given these things careful consideration, we ask you to explore them again. The process may give you the opportunity to fine-tune your thinking, confirm what you already know or shift your perspective, and view "the business" in a new light.

Once you've done the following inventory, we'll ask you to think about your career in the greater scheme of things and look at how you approach your work in regard to its impact on others.

For some actors, these might be radical concepts, and for others, these ideas might already be the backbone of an existing or emerging philosophy about life. Perhaps you'll discover that you fall someplace in between. Wherever you are on this continuum, keep an open mind and you will see how these ideas and principles are intrinsically linked and interconnected.

Learn what it is you are. Learn how to be who you are.
Implement what and who you are into the moment.
Do this on stage, and in life. The rest will follow.
— Ryan Graham, actor

Your Personal Inventory

Exercise Part I: **Fill out the following questionnaire. Try to do it in one sitting. Answer with the first thought that comes to mind (utilize blank pages at the end of the book as necessary). If you need to go back and revise, that's great. Spend time on it. Consider it thoughtfully. It will probably take you 45 minutes to an hour.**

Describe yourself physically—height, weight, hair color, eye color, etc.

This is what I like about my looks . . .

I wish I looked like . . .

This is what I would love to change about my looks . . .

Here's what I don't like about my looks . . .

These are the positive things I can do to refine my appearance (grooming, exercise, diet, haircut, etc.) . . .

Here are the reasons I don't do the above . . .

How would people describe me simply by looking at me?

What do my nonverbal signals say about me?

The hardest thing to accept about my appearance is . . .

My greatest physical asset is . . .

Based on my physical appearance, the kinds of characters I play are . . .

If appearance had no impact, I would love to play these kinds of characters . . .

What can I do to make myself more castable in the roles I would like to play?

My greatest asset as a person is . . .

The fears I reveal about myself are . . .

The fears I can't reveal about myself are . . .

The situation(s) where I feel the most confident is/are . . .

Because . . .

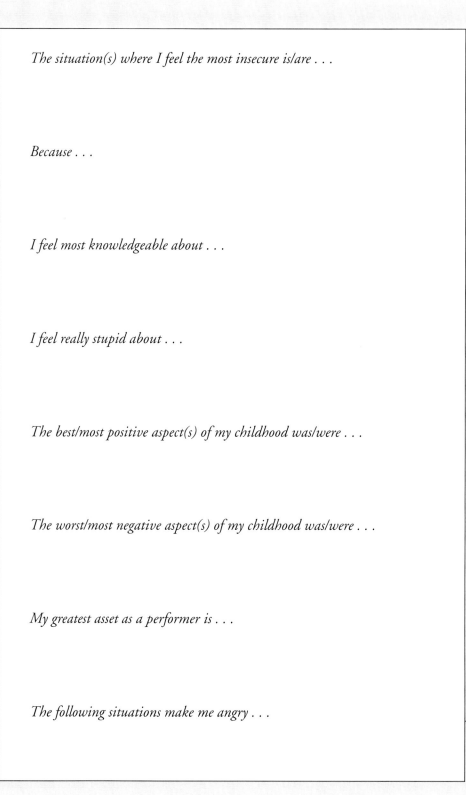

The situation(s) where I feel the most insecure is/are . . .

Because . . .

I feel most knowledgeable about . . .

I feel really stupid about . . .

The best/most positive aspect(s) of my childhood was/were . . .

The worst/most negative aspect(s) of my childhood was/were . . .

My greatest asset as a performer is . . .

The following situations make me angry . . .

The following situations make me laugh . . .

The following situations make me defensive . . .

To me, risk taking means . . .

Things that I don't want people to know about me are . . .

My attitudes about sex and sexuality are . . .

My comfort level with my own sexuality is (how do I feel about myself as a sexual being?) . . .

To me, the word fearless means . . .

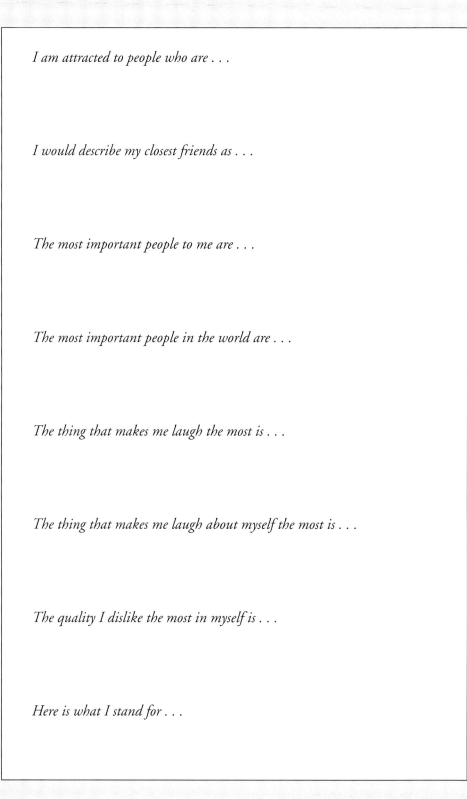

I am attracted to people who are . . .

I would describe my closest friends as . . .

The most important people to me are . . .

The most important people in the world are . . .

The thing that makes me laugh the most is . . .

The thing that makes me laugh about myself the most is . . .

The quality I dislike the most in myself is . . .

Here is what I stand for . . .

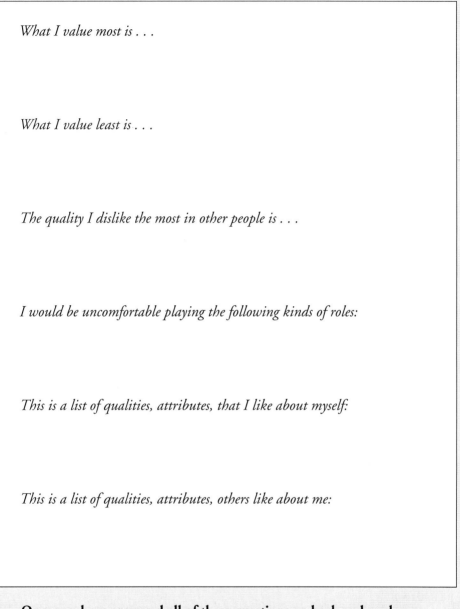

What I value most is . . .

What I value least is . . .

The quality I dislike the most in other people is . . .

I would be uncomfortable playing the following kinds of roles:

This is a list of qualities, attributes, that I like about myself:

This is a list of qualities, attributes, others like about me:

Once you have answered all of these questions go back and read your responses. Take some time to reflect—maybe a day, even a week. Come back and read it again. You may want to ask yourself these questions throughout your career.

Self-awareness is critical for any actor. Asking yourself difficult questions, reflecting on aspects of yourself that might challenge you, and assessing your strengths are vital to the process of being your own CEO. Yes, you are the only person who can run your own business. Therefore, you are the head of your "company." You may not have thought of it that way but once you do, you will see the importance of taking ownership of your career. You need to understand the areas where you excel as well as the areas that give you trouble. Understanding yourself will allow you to develop strategies that play to your strengths. You will also be able to formulate solutions for overcoming weaknesses.

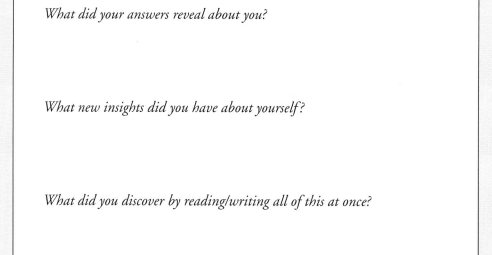

Insights from Your Inventory

Exercise Part II: **Spend a few minutes writing your responses to the following questions:**

What did your answers reveal about you?

What new insights did you have about yourself?

What did you discover by reading/writing all of this at once?

Further Reflection . . .

- In what ways did you find this exercise useful as a *person?*
- How did you find it useful as an *actor?*

> Know that the sun comes up every day and that you have the chance to move forward every day. You are responsible for your career and your happiness. There is no one way to be successful. If one way does not work, try another. Anything is possible.
> — Matthew Prescott, dancer/choreographer

EXPLORING YOUR MOTIVATION

It's important to examine the motivation behind your desire for success. The following exercise will help you explore what fuels your motivation.

Your Motivation to Be a Successful Actor

Exercise: **This is a stream of consciousness writing exercise. You don't need to write in complete sentences—no one is going to see this but you. Don't stop and ponder an idea or try to frame it precisely. Write down whatever comes to mind. There are no wrong answers. Time yourself and write for five minutes without stopping (utilize blank pages in the back of the book as necessary). Start now.**

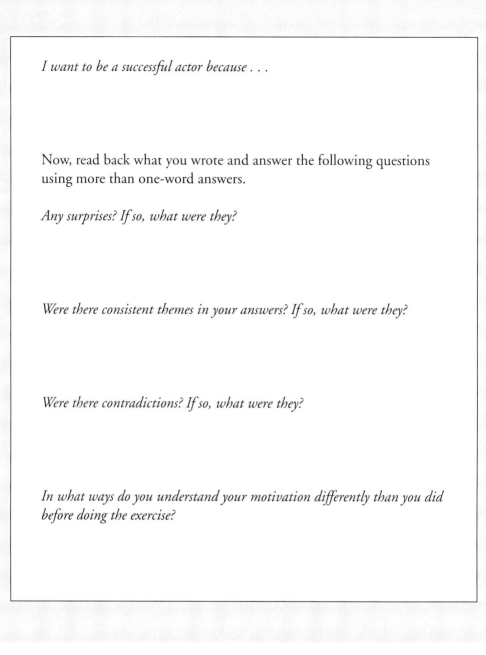

I want to be a successful actor because . . .

Now, read back what you wrote and answer the following questions using more than one-word answers.

Any surprises? If so, what were they?

Were there consistent themes in your answers? If so, what were they?

Were there contradictions? If so, what were they?

In what ways do you understand your motivation differently than you did before doing the exercise?

Take a closer look at your responses. Some of your motivations may include virtuous and impressive reasons for wanting to be a successful actor, but you may notice less ideal motivators as well. For example, did some of your writing reflect sentiments about finding success as a means of "showing" someone you can "make it" or getting revenge on someone who you think wronged you? If you're chasing your success to "show him/her/them" or "prove I'm better than him/her/them," you risk tying your success and happiness to those people. There is no denying that "showing someone" can be a powerful motivator—one that ignites your energy and passion and can lead to success. When important people in our lives (or people we perceive to be important), withhold their support, diminish our aspirations, or undermine us with their comments, they can stir an overwhelming need to prove them wrong. Some people find pleasure in belittling others because they somehow feel it will make them look better. Some people project their values on others, and see little validity in life as an actor. The person who was mocked in high school, or told he wasn't good enough, or whose parents or loved ones called his or her dream of being an actor silly and frivolous may feel the need to "prove" something to others.

The negative feelings that arise from such motivating forces give our detractors a lot of power. Will "proving" or "showing them" win their approval or acceptance? Will it somehow make them look stupid? What do we really prove if our motivation is tied solely to these people who hold us hostage with their doubt and disapproval? How much time will it take and how much of your career will you spend before you decide to "prove it" to yourself and let go of the need to show "them"? The goal is to move to a place of confidence and self-worth—to an emotional place where "I'll prove it to you" no longer carries any weight.

For some, motivation is tied to a desire for celebrity, fame, and money (there's nothing wrong with that), but if the desire is rooted in the belief that those things bring self-worth, then all the accomplishments in the world won't fill that void. Money and fame don't guarantee self-esteem and fulfillment. Take a look at the number of famous people who struggle with alcohol, drug addiction, and depression. There are countless crash-and-burn stories of Hollywood stars who appeared to have everything but were completely self-destructive.

> If you're going into acting to become rich and/or famous,
> I guarantee you will be disappointed. Those are the
> wrong reasons, period. Less than one percent of all actors
> out there reach that kind of recognition. You should go
> into acting as a profession only if your heart tells you
> that you truly can't imagine doing anything else. It's that
> kind of passion that will keep you afloat during the
> dry spells and the rejections and all the other rough spots
> that may or may not fall into your lap along the way.
> — Stephen Wallem, actor

We are idealistic enough to assume that your motivations are not grounded in greed, manipulation, and hunger for power. If they are, then you are destined for a career where you may be feared, disliked, mistrusted, and even sabotaged. Make a commitment to use your gifts wisely and constructively. Think of the criminal who spends countless hours making a counterfeit $100 bill. Imagine what that person could do with his or her brilliant artistic gifts instead of wasting them on deception.

Carefully examine your motivations. If they resonate with any of the scenarios we described above, make a choice to work through those issues. Awareness is the first step that leads to change. This book raises these issues so that we can raise your awareness. It's impossible for you to change something about yourself without being aware of it.

Issues surrounding motivation, success, and self-esteem can be complex. We're not therapists, but we believe that an actor's mental health is as important as his or her physical and vocal health. Unearthing the path to an emotionally balanced life isn't a luxury—it's a necessity. If you need help, get it. Release the notion that only "sick people" ask for help. Avail yourself of the resources at your disposal—books, tapes, school counseling centers, twelve-step programs, churches, etc.

If you're serious about having a happy, satisfying career, you'll find the time and energy to examine and develop strategies and coping mechanisms that empower you to deal with these challenges. It will make your life manageable and, in the end, make you a much more effective and grounded actor.

Further Reflection . . .
- **How did articulating your motivation help?**
- **What were the challenges in putting this in words?**

Discover something you can do that sets you apart,
can be done anywhere, anytime, and charge people for it.
Keep your days and nights open and be willing to live
with the bare essentials. Make your craft the priority.
— Tania Richard, actor/playwright

Dispatches from the Field—Carl

A Story of Misguided Motivation. I was educated at Northwestern University—an institution that is famous for producing many successful members of the entertainment industry. I went to school with people who went on to achieve not only success but also a good deal of fame. I was convinced that true success was about achieving what my classmates achieved, and until I had a high profile position in "the business" I was not successful. I finished my undergraduate studies with a background in both theatre and education. I was always somewhat reticent about being a teacher. I was haunted by the expression "those who can't do, teach."

Yet throughout my career, I was unable to walk away from my many unglamorous jobs as a teacher. No matter what type of theatre job I had, I always had a second job teaching. My teaching jobs gave me tremendous satisfaction and energy. To this day, I am still in contact with many former students. Some of those relationships date back more than twenty years. Yet, in spite of both my success and fulfillment as a teacher, I needed to prove that I was a "winner." It didn't matter that eventually I ran the theatre program in one of the top high schools in the nation that had two theatre facilities and an enrollment of more than one hundred students a year. People would ask me what I did for a living and I would say, "I'm a school teacher." One day a friend asked why I put it like that. He told me that my accomplishments as an educator were impressive, that my success at the school was noteworthy. I was unable to see myself as anything more than some teacher who couldn't take what the theatre had to dish out.

Hopefully, you can see my misplaced motivation. My desire to achieve success in the theatre didn't come from a positive place. The success I did achieve was somewhat hollow because I thought it couldn't compare to my successful classmates. At the time, I was unable to see that mine was a different kind of success. I spent many years not minding the edge and wandered into the abyss of negative thinking. Fortunately, with age comes wisdom. There are few things in life that give me more joy and fulfillment than working with my students in a classroom or in rehearsal for a production. I wouldn't trade these experiences for an Oscar or a Broadway show. My work as an educator is enormously fulfilling, and I stopped making excuses for my desire to teach. Teaching, not acting or fame, is my passion and with it comes enormous satisfaction.

So, ask yourself if your motivation is tied to someone else's definition of success.

CONFIDENCE

In order to be successful you must be confident in your talent, abilities, and work ethic. You can't survive in the arts without confidence. When you are confident, you understand your strengths and challenges. When you are confident, you are not shaken by external factors or opinions. Confident people carry themselves like they are of value. Confident people learn from their mistakes and are not undone by them. Make sure you don't mistake confidence with arrogance. We are not endorsing arrogance. Arrogance is an overinflated sense of self-worth and an overbearing pride that results in an air of superiority.

Recognize the difference between feeling confident and being a bottomless pit that needs constant praise and approval. We're sure you've been around people who make it "all about them." What they don't understand is that it's not about them. It's about them in context. It's about them in relation to others, to the rest of the world. No one is God's only gift to acting. No one person defines an industry or a profession. We don't exist in a vacuum, and our presence and success on this planet are connected to thousands of other people (seen and unseen) who contribute to our existence. It's both humbling and vital to embrace that.

A successful approach to living a fulfilled life as an actor is to manage the challenges and complexities of being a freelance artist with self-awareness, a positive mind-set, and a generous spirit. The ongoing reality check that includes examining your motivations is one of the challenges and payoffs of MTE. As your career evolves, you need to keep your eye on the edge and keep your motivation coming from a confident, positive, and hopeful place.

In order to fully understand your motivation, you must ask yourself: "How much do I want to be an actor?" We assume you want to be a successful, fulfilled actor, but the real question is, "how much?" Being an actor will require a tremendous amount of self-motivation and drive. It is not enough to merely want to be an actor. You will have to want it enough that you will make the necessary sacrifices and trade-offs that your career demands. The story below is a good example of someone who understands and makes those trade-offs, sacrifices and demands.

Dispatches from the Field—Carl

A successful actor, who was an American University alum, conducted a master class for my students. He worked in Europe and had become a "star" in Germany. He even had a fan club. In order to fulfill his passion and realize his dreams, he was willing to make many sacrifices. He pointed out that his social life was incredibly compromised when he was in a show. While he was performing, most of the world was out socializing. A good portion of his day was devoted to working out, resting his voice (he sang many roles in vocally demanding musicals), getting enough sleep, and tending to the business of his career. Often there wasn't a lot of time for a social life. But performing was fulfilling and satisfying, and he continued to find joy in it. He was willing to take disciplined actions because he was passionate about his work, motivated to find work, and driven to remain successful and focused. In his mind, there was a clear distinction between trade-offs and "sacrificing for his art." He was an upbeat, positive and engaging person, and didn't view his compromises as sacrifices. While he admitted that it was not easy, he also said he couldn't imagine a more wonderful life.

It's not uncommon for me to talk with recent grads about their careers. The ones who are not having success often make excuses, but it is easy to see that they are not driven. They don't want it enough. One of my students graduated and immediately found work. He landed a few acting jobs right out of school. When the last of the jobs was about to conclude, he asked me to meet him for lunch. He told me that he didn't know what to do to get work and worried he wasn't going to work in the near future. He seemed somewhat paralyzed. I asked him to describe the ways he was making opportunities, finding auditions and building relationships with theatre professionals. His answer was that he wasn't good at that, didn't enjoy doing it, and as a result, couldn't get motivated enough to do it. I pointed out that he was an incredibly disciplined and motivated person when it came to swimming and playing tennis. He made the time, enjoyed the process, and looked forward to doing these activities. A little further into our conversation it became clear that he had little faith in himself and was afraid that he wasn't good enough—this in spite of the fact that he had been hired by professional theatres immediately after graduating. His self-doubt killed his drive and derailed his success. He was convinced he wouldn't succeed and was afraid to fail, so he put up a defense and made excuses. In the end, he didn't want it enough to fight the destructive internal demons.

While this isn't a particularly hopeful, uplifting story I believe it's an important illustration of the complexities of disciplined thought, honest self-assessment, and positively aligned motivation. The good news for this actor is that he decided to see a therapist who helped him work through the issues that were undermining him.

Quality of life should be priority #1. Shows come and go . . .
the high of getting cast in your dream role is fantastic, but has
an expiration date. The knowledge that you are happy, doing
something that truly fulfills you, independent of whether or not
you are doing what others expect you to be doing, is what
you will take with you when the "curtain closes."
Remember, ultimately you are accountable only to you.
— Javier Rivera, actor

DEFINING FULFILLMENT

This chapter is about understanding yourself and examining the factors that drive you toward your career goals. One of those factors is the desire for success and fulfillment. In this next section, we're going to explore the elements of fulfillment that are foundational to your definition of success.

Visualizing Your Fulfillment

Exercise: **The following is a guided meditation exercise to help you identify career fulfillment. Either have someone read the guided meditation to you out loud or use a recording of yourself reading it. Be sure whoever reads it talks slowly and in a calming, encouraging tone. Pause after reading every sentence. This will allow you a moment to mentally absorb and respond to each question or direction. As you do the meditation, make a mental note of the satisfying feelings and emotional states you experience. Have paper and pen ready to write down your impressions afterward.**

Before you begin, read the guided meditation below. Then decide on a specific event or a moment that elicits a tremendous sense of professional, artistic fulfillment—an event or experience that is a source of joy, happiness, and energy for you. This can be an event from your past or one that you hope will happen in the future. This can be a onetime event or ongoing situation. It can be a place you're working, or a setting in which you receive an award or have an opportunity to express yourself as an artist. If it's an experience you've had in the past, make sure it's a moment when you felt that you were completely satisfied and fulfilled. Make it concrete. Be sure it's a moment that you can picture in your mind's eye.

Find a comfortable place where you can sit or lie down, undisturbed, for about five minutes. Listen to the following mediation:

Close your eyes and relax. Pay attention to your breathing and take deep slow breaths. Take in a gentle, deep breath . . . and let it out. Again, breathe in . . . and let all the air go out. One more time—breathe in . . . and let the breath go out. Be aware of the rhythm of your breath. Clear your mind and focus on your breathing and the sound of my voice.

Think about the moment you identified. See yourself in that setting. What do you see? What do the surroundings look like? What objects are around you? What colors or light do you see? Who do you see there with you? What are you doing as this event unfolds? What is happening as you watch this event? What are the people saying to you and about you? How do you feel about those comments? Connect to all the positive feelings you experience. What do you feel? What does it feel like to have arrived at this goal or dream? What is it like to feel this sense of accomplishment? Take a few moments to connect to your mental and emotional state. Make sure you continue to breathe deeply. Let the feelings fill you with happiness, pride, joy, and fulfillment. Allow this image to play out in your mind. See the moment clearly. Put yourself in that place, in that moment. Keep breathing deeply. Bring it into focus so you can connect with the positive energy it brings you. Allow that energy to engulf you so that you experience it in your mind and your body. Feel the satisfaction and joy you get when you are fulfilled. What's happening to bring you to this state? How did you get to such a satisfying state of being? Continue to breathe and experience this event. Now allow your breathing to bring you back to the awareness of your body and your current surroundings. Take in a deep breath. Let it out. In again. Let it out. One last time, and let it out. When you are ready, open your eyes.

Explain what you felt. Don't think about it. Just write for 5 minutes.

Identifying Your Personal Fulfillment Needs (PFNs)

Professional or artistic fulfillment is usually defined by the successful achievement of a goal, but the definition of fulfillment doesn't always include the path to that success. We believe that the journey can be as artistically fulfilling as the outcome. The process can be equally, if not more, rewarding than the outcome. It's not only what you achieved, but it's how you achieved it. The questions below were designed with that broader notion of fulfillment in mind. Notice that we're asking you to examine both internal and external contributors to your fulfillment.

All of the questions may not apply to the event you visualized, but they may inspire your definition of fulfillment. Try to answer all of them.

What did you accomplish? What did that accomplishment mean to you? What was its significance?

What skills were you utilizing? What abilities were you demonstrating?

In what ways were your passions engaged and ignited?

In what ways were your body, mind, and spirit engaged?

In what ways were you challenged? How did you meet the challenges? How did you succeed?

In what ways did you explore or realize your potential?

Did you take risks? How did that risk-taking pay off?

In what ways were you creative?

In what ways were you innovative?

In what ways did you utilize the resources available to you?

In what ways did you feel confident?

In what ways did your achievement reflect your personal/professional values?

Describe the type environment where the fulfilling event took place. (Not the physical environment as much as the tone, vibe, and atmosphere.)

How were you received? How did others react to you?

In what ways did your interactions with others contribute to your fulfillment?

In what ways did you feel connected to others?

Describe any positive outcomes in regard to your relationships with others involved.

In what ways did you inspire others?

In what ways were you inspired?

In what ways did you contribute to the whole?

Review your answers. Spend a few minutes considering each response.

Now take five minutes and write your definition of professional fulfillment. Write for the full five minutes without stopping. You can edit your definition later.

Congratulations. You have taken a first step toward understanding and articulating your personal fulfillment needs.

Dispatches from the Field—Carl

The first time I did this exercise, Lori was leading a group of my students through the visualization. I did it along with the students. What I visualized was the first day of rehearsal for a play I had written. I saw a group of respectful, bright, passionate theatre artists taking ownership of the production and bringing their creative energies to the play I wrote. What I experienced was a sense of collaboration in its purest state. People listening, sharing, exchanging, and contributing a host of varied talents, experiences, and perspectives to develop a production that was far better than anything any single person could have created alone. What was enlightening was not about getting the play produced but realizing that if I'm going to be professionally fulfilled, I need to feel collaborative in the truest sense of the word. While it is something I always knew, I had never articulated it so simply. I always said I valued collaboration and found a truly collaborative process satisfying. I never thought of it as a need connected to my professional fulfillment and satisfaction.

The *way* we live our lives can be as vital to our fulfillment as our achievements and success themselves. Many actors get frustrated because they put so much focus on their big goals that they don't recognize fulfillment when it shows up in smaller ways. They focus only on the fact that they still haven't achieved their goal. They feel empty-handed. They neglect to find the joy in the journey and then feel like quitting. While it is certainly true that your goal should motivate you to reach it, it's important to appreciate and enjoy the road that gets you there. The secret is to celebrate the small victories while you're on your way to the bigger goal. If you don't, you might experience a long, dry spell or perhaps give up before you get to the pot of gold at the end of that rainbow.

The secret is to enjoy the small victories while you're on your way to the bigger goal.

People have a choice in the way they deal with what's in front of them. Remember, you are the CEO. You are in charge of your career and of maintaining your confidence and self-esteem. Now that you have identified your PFNs, it will be easier to acknowledge them when they show up in your life and career. The needs and values you described can be met and experienced throughout your life, not just in the particular event you visualized in the guided meditation exercise. Life affords us the luxury of experiencing these feelings over and over in a variety of contexts.

You will find that you experience the feelings associated with the PFNs to greater or lesser degrees in the course of an average week. You may not feel all of them at once or as intensely as you will when your goal becomes reality, but you can feel them nonetheless. Here's an exercise to help you do it.

Putting Your PFNs into Motion

Exercise: **Revisit your PFNs from the previous exercise.**

- Choose one PFN per day.
- Write the PFN on a few pieces of paper or Post-it notes.
- Place the notes where you will see them. This could be on your bathroom mirror, in your wallet, on your computer screen, the fridge, your bedside table, above the TV screen, or maybe stuck to your credit card, subway pass, or ID . . . have fun with it!
- An easy way to remind yourself to look for evidence of your PFN each day is to add a **physical reminder** by making a **physical change** to break up your routine. This will help remind your brain to be aware of consistently incorporating the change. For instance, wear your watch on a different wrist. Put your wallet in a different pocket. Do something that will make you constantly aware that something is physically different. Every time you notice the watch on the other wrist, allow it to be a reminder that you're supposed to think about the feeling of satisfaction from the PFN that you have chosen for that day.
- At the end of the day, ask yourself when you experienced your PFN.
- Do this for five days this week—one day for each PFN.

Here's an example: Let's say your PFN is to feel "affirmed." At the end of the day you would look back over that day's events and identify the times when you felt affirmed. Did your boss tell you that you did a good job? Did you get a large tip from a customer when you were tending bar? Did someone compliment you? Whether the feelings you are looking for show up in the simple and mundane moments of your life or in earth shattering ways, your awareness of them will keep you feeling fulfilled and fuel you on to your goals. Keep track of them.

While the affirmation you get from winning an Academy Award is different from the affirmation you get on a successful audition, they are still affirmations. If you set yourself up to feel affirmation only through that Oscar, the time between now and then could be a difficult, unsatisfying experience. Remember it's about the journey not just the destination.

Further Reflection . . .

- **Where did you discover your instances when your personal fulfillment needs were met?**
- **Were there any surprises? Describe them.**
- **What, if any, impact did this have on your outlook?**

Dispatches from the Field—Lori

I grew up in North Dakota and started competing in talent shows when I was 12 years old. Early wins really helped me believe that I could be a professional performer. My mother fiercely believed in my talent. But, let me just say that I couldn't have started out with fewer contacts and connections in "the business." First of all, there weren't any professional theatres in the area. But my mother never saw that as a hindrance. She recognized my gift as a singer and found venues where I could perform. She inspired me by saying that my current experiences were all "stepping-stones" on a path to where I wanted to go. Her "can-do" attitude always made things seem possible.

After college, I made my way from Wichita to Chicago and finally to New York City. None of it happened overnight, and sometimes it seemed like my dream would never come true. With perseverance and discipline, roles and opportunities continued to come my way. After performing in some fabulous off-Broadway shows, I was cast in the national tour of Mamma Mia! After a year of touring, a spot opened up in

New York, and they asked if I would like to join the Broadway production. Eventually, I got to perform the role of Donna (think Meryl Streep's role in the movie). There I was, the girl from North Dakota playing the leading role—talk about a dream coming true!

Once the whirlwind of excitement faded and I settled into the routine of doing my job on Broadway, I realized that my life had been about one goal—a goal I had now achieved. It was an amazing feeling, and it truly filled a need. I got to Broadway. But now what? I had a lot of career ahead of me, but I hadn't taken the time to discover what it meant to be a fulfilled actor once I had achieved my concrete goal. I felt like I was staring at a blank canvas. So, I asked myself what steps I needed to take to grow as an actor. What needs still had to be met? What needs did I have to continue to meet? I had to be willing to rework my goals and view them in light of how they worked together with my personal and professional needs. I am definitely finding more joy in the journey as I allow myself to find fulfillment in the process, not just the outcome.

Dispatches from the Field—Carl

If you spend your life in search of the needs *that constitute your personal satisfaction and fulfillment, then you will discover fulfillment more frequently and in more places. You'll find satisfaction in the actions that get you to your goal, as well as in the goal itself. Have you ever experienced the following: You are in a production. Through the rehearsal and performance process you build wonderful relationships; you do good work; your work is affirmed by others, as well as yourself; you enjoy going to rehearsals and the performances. Then the show closes. You don't have those daily encounters with those people you enjoy. You feel as though a part of you is missing. There is even a short mourning period. You realize how much you enjoyed the time you spent on that project, how good it made you feel, and now you're feeling let down and perhaps somewhat empty. When we experience joy, fulfillment, and satisfaction, it's important to recognize it in the present, in the moment. When I direct a production and the process is going well, with a great collaborative spirit among the artists involved, I often remind the cast to recognize the moment. Realize the joy as you experience it, rather than living your life in hindsight—looking back and saying, "I didn't realize how wonderful that was! Too bad it's over." There's nothing wrong with feeling sad or let down when it's over, but make sure you haven't allowed a positive experience to pass by without acknowledging it as you experience it. I try to remind myself, while I'm in the process, of all of the ways in which I am satisfied by the process.*

MTE requires you to be the manager of your fulfillment rather than waiting passively to experience something positive. If you allow yourself to experience fulfillment in multiple ways, you'll pave a more positive pathway that can potentially impact many areas of your personal and professional life.

Pursuing goals derived from your personal fulfillment needs can lead to a more gratifying journey. When you experience fulfillment in both large and small ways, you create momentum that will help you move forward through life's obstacles. Seeking fulfillment means you know what's important. It means you know what you need. As you pursue fulfillment, you begin minding the edge of a career that can sustain itself over many years.

CHOOSE TO BE FULFILLED

If your definition of success is driven by fulfillment as well as concrete goals, then you already have a greater chance of lasting happiness. Defining your fulfillment (PFNs) and deciding that you'll be fulfilled is where it all begins. While most actors readily admit that they would like to have fulfilling careers, many create obstacles so that they can't feel satisfaction. For many people in highly competitive careers there is no amount of success that can bring them happiness and peace of mind.

You have to decide that you deserve to be fulfilled. You can set yourself up to win or to struggle and fail. We'd like you to try viewing your career as a *challenge* rather than a *struggle*. There is a difference. If you consider what's implied by both words, you can see it. Athletic competitions are often called "challenges." When you're challenged, there is an implication that the situation or contest you're participating in presents the opportunity for you to come out on top, to succeed. This concept isn't implicit in the word "struggle." *Challenge* yourself to be fulfilled.

Have you ever come across actors who are unable to be happy no matter what happens to them? For example, let's take a look at

"Brenda." Shortly after Brenda arrives in New York, she books a job as an understudy in an off-Broadway show. Does Brenda celebrate her accomplishment? No, she immediately feels jealous of the actor who is cast in the role she's understudying. Brenda is certain she could do a better job. She begins to panic about understudy rehearsals, whether or not the director will notice her and cast her in a larger role someday, and whether or not she'll get a chance to perform the role. The male understudy is really attractive. Brenda hopes he's straight. Maybe she can start a relationship with him. She hopes he likes her. If he's straight he probably has a girlfriend. This is Brenda's constant inner chatter and worry. She is so preoccupied with anything but her current success that she deprives herself of the opportunity to be happy and fulfilled. Brenda doesn't really believe that she deserves to be happy. Logically, if Brenda can't feel good about a step along the way to her goal, how will she ever allow herself to feel fulfilled once she does reach her dream?

The notion that a "true artist" is a starving, struggling artist is a concept that's been reflected in our culture for many years. The opera *La Boehme* and its adapted hit musical *Rent* romanticizes the image of the starving artist. Beautiful death scenes at the end of the play bring tears to the audience. Yes, there is the notion that these people have each other and that's all that matters, and at its core there is great truth in that. But think about this in practical terms—dying because you can't afford to take care of yourself is not a life anyone wants to lead. You may not require lots of possessions, an upscale home, and a fancy wardrobe, but no one wants to worry about paying the rent and covering the cost of basic needs. There's nothing romantic in that.

The brilliant painter George Seurat didn't achieve the kind of success he deserved during his lifetime. His genius was recognized only after his death. You can't be a posthumous stage actor with the world discovering how talented you are once you're dead. So ask yourself—is an unsuccessful life really more fulfilling?

We are not suggesting that just because you decide to be fulfilled, satisfaction will magically arrive at your front door while you're on Facebook. Creating a successful, fulfilling career is challenging, but well-trained, disciplined professionals can achieve it when they decide that they deserve it.

To achieve professional fulfillment, actors need to keep their eyes on the goal and silence the negative voices—the detractors that can derail you and get in your way. These detractors take all sorts of forms: family members, friends, partners, and past events. Some actors use old, negating voices from the past as motivation in the present. As we've discussed, these powerfully motivating forces are driven by negative feelings and thoughts.

Minding the edge demands that you examine and update your fulfillment needs and your motivations as you change and grow. The needs that you were trying to fulfill when you were ten years old are

One of the greatest (and most profound) gifts someone gave me was in the form of a short statement delivered my way after I'd spewed out a five-minute rant on why I wasn't more successful in my career than I thought I should be. The Gift Giver lifted a glass of gin to her lips, took a long, luxuriating sip, swallowed without flinching, locked her eyes on me and said, "Nobody asked you to be a writer." After the sting wore off (and I picked my ego up off the floor), I got to thinking: she's absolutely right. Nobody forced me to be a writer. Nobody put a gun to my head and said, *"You will be a writer or else!"* It's a choice. It's a daily choice that I make for myself. I consciously choose to do this every day of every month of every year. That's true for all artists. "Nobody asked you to be an actor." It's your choice, and when you recognize that statement for its resonant truth, you'll have grown up a little bit to assume the responsibility for your career—with all its highs and its lows. And that's where the responsibility belongs—on you.

— Gary Garrison, playwright

probably not your current needs. And most likely, what motivated you at age ten is not what drives you now.

Reflecting on Past Fulfillments

Exercise Part I: **Think about the satisfaction you've had in your life thus far. Did it happen by chance? Was everything handed to you, or did you have to earn your success? Do those successes feel rewarding? Now that you've identified your personal fulfillment needs, we'd like you to reflect on moments and events in your life that have been fulfilling.**

In your journal, make a list of three events or moments that were fulfilling. These can be personal or professional experiences. They can be recent or from your past.

Under each experience, describe five major action steps you took in order to achieve that success.

Compare your three events.
- *What actions were the same or similar?*

- *What motivated you to achieve the success? How much did you want it?*

- *Did any of the actions take discipline?*

- *In what way did they take discipline?*

- *How could you repeat those actions in order to achieve that fulfillment again?*

- *How did you celebrate these successes?*

It's important to realize that you already possess a variety of skills, disciplines, and talents that contribute to your ability to find fulfillment. Now that you have defined fulfillment for your career, you can take the necessary action steps to make it happen.

> Seek mentors that are where you want to be and have been
> where you are. Broaden your horizons and assist a producer
> or a choreographer or a director or a casting director.
> See things from a different point of view.
> — Matt Lenz, director

Fulfillment in Others You Admire

Exercise Part II: **Think of two people currently in your life whom you view as personally and/or professionally fulfilled.**

Step 1. Answer the following:
Why do you think they are fulfilled?

How do you think they achieved fulfillment?

How are you similar in your own actions or attitudes to these two people?

Step 2. Now that you've made your hypothesis about why these two people are fulfilled, it's time to do the research and test your theory. Take notes when you contact both of these people and ask them:

How do you define fulfillment?

What did you do to achieve fulfillment?

What contributes to your continued fulfillment and success?

Step 3. Compare your list of the actions you took to create your fulfillment with the answers from the two people you interviewed. Ask yourself:

How is your vision of fulfillment similar to theirs?

How is it different?

What aspects of their fulfillment aren't on your lists?

After talking to others, what insights did you have about your fulfillment and about the course of action you need to take to get there?

Could you revise or refine your PFNs based on these insights? If so, how?

Minding the edge means developing your ability to monitor your actions in pursuit of your fulfillment and success. Don't expect anyone but *you* to take charge of this. You need to be in charge of your fulfillment rather than leaving it in the hands of others. Now that you've defined fulfillment for yourself and examined it in others, we'll help you design strategies and action steps that can set you up for success and place you on the path to a more fulfilling career.

Chapter 3

The Disciplined Actor

Taking Control

> We've all heard stories about actors who've never studied, who auditioned only one time and became a star shortly after, who always showed up late for rehearsals and didn't get fired because they were so brilliant that the producer or director was willing to put up with their poor behavior, who showed up drunk or stoned, who just happened to be in the right place at the right time and boom, they got the starring role in a major motion picture; yes, we've all heard those stories, and every once in a very rare while they may be true, but I don't suggest or support that you follow any of those paths. Nothing takes the place of discipline, hard work, and respect for your fellow artists.
>
> — Gary Dontzig, writer/producer

*I*t is difficult to be successful in this business without discipline. Disciplined thoughts and actions move you toward your goals and needs. Discipline is devoting time and energy to generate opportunities rather than waiting passively for them to happen. A disciplined actor is proactive rather than reactive. This behavior allows actors to MTE as they create steps toward success.

There are many myths in our society about being an actor. Some of these stories are legendary—that someone is going to "discover" you when you're sitting in a diner. If you don't know that story, read about Lana Turner—that happens to only one in a million actors. Many young actors believe that someone else (an agent or manager) is going to do all the work for them while they sip cool drinks by the pool. Yet, even if this were true, would you really want someone else calling the shots? Many actors of "megastar proportions" start their own production companies and consistently create new work for themselves because they are willing to take the disciplined actions necessary to move their careers in a direction *they* desire. Again, discipline is the key to finding and making your own work.

It's not uncommon for people outside "the business" to think that acting is easy. Just get up there and do it, right? The famous actor and teacher Uta Hagen wrote the highly regarded book *Respect for Acting*. You may have read it for one of your acting classes or on your own. She observes that people look at actors and think, "I could do that." Hagen uses her book to illustrate how labor-intensive the process is. She likens acting to other artistic disciplines. Unless you had extensive training as a dancer, you would think it ridiculous if we took you to a rehearsal at the American Ballet Theatre and told you to fill in for a role in *The Nutcracker*. If you're not a highly trained dancer, you don't look at ballet dancers and assume, "I could do that." The craft, the art, of acting, is a discipline and requires a lifetime of hard work. The same is true with managing your career and your success. It won't happen unless you make it happen. Work will not just show up at your door while you do your warm-ups or practice your monologues.

Actors need to use the resources around them to create opportunities. Sometimes those opportunities may be hidden in your current surroundings. It is only by diligently leaving no stone unturned that you generate possibilities. If you do the work, you'll discover that the effort puts you ahead. Invest your energy in the process as well as the end goal. You won't always know how it will come back to you, but you will have used your energy for advancing your career.

> The secret of success in acting is to work harder than everyone else. Once you leave school, no one is going to push you to be all you can be. You must find a way to motivate yourself every day. Remember that acting is your job. It is the best job in the world, but it still is a job. However, unlike other jobs, if you ever start hating this job, you must find another career. If you don't love what you do, what is the point?
> — Karl Kippola, actor

As an actor, you need to learn to cope with the stresses of this business and that requires discipline. Why do actors need so much more discipline than other professionals? Think of it this way—actors live their lives in a way that most people consider an emergency. Looking for work or changing jobs is viewed, by many, as a major stressor. Actors are constantly engaged in a process that most people experience every few years, if at all.

Ask your nonactor friends how often they:

- Update their resumes
- Interview for jobs
- Live in a state of limbo as they wait to hear from a prospective employer
- Face the rejection of not getting a job

Interestingly enough, actors must continually face another major stressor, losing a job. Yes, actors are incredibly brave, but all these stressors mean that actors have to cultivate the courage to practice their art *and* the discipline to manage their businesses.

Actors are continually asking someone to hire them, and that can make anyone feel powerless. MTE means you create a disciplined mind-set that empowers you to be your own business owner. As the

CEO of your own company, you are not merely reacting to the ups and downs of being chosen for other people's projects, *you* are in control of your vision and your career plan. You will be *in charge* of your time, efforts, and resources as you seek and create work. You will be *in charge* of the relationships with those who will eventually work for you (agents and managers). You will feel *empowered* to meet the people with whom you would like to work as well as continue to remain connected to your current business contacts.

By MTE, you can stand at the precipice and see the possibilities in front of you, rather than remain safely on the sidelines living a vision others have created for you or even worse being immobilized by your fears and doubts. Assessing your fulfillment is a challenge, as is remaining focused on your objective. When you're starting out, all of this might be accomplished while you juggle a temporary job (or several temp jobs) and simultaneously look for acting work. But, if you're minding the edge, you'll be on top of your game and managing your expectations along with your vision of success and fulfillment.

It should go without saying that coping with the stress of "the business" requires an actor to live a healthy lifestyle; exercise is a great stress reducer. There are lots of resources that can help illuminate the path to a healthy lifestyle, but living that lifestyle requires *discipline*.

Dispatches from the Field—Lori

One day, a long time ago, I was sitting in the front seat of my old Impala in the empty parking lot of a grocery store in Wichita, Kansas. I was fresh out of college with my Performing Arts BA, wearing a business suit and selling office machinery (something I knew little about) and thinking of reasons not to go on my next cold call (that is, walking into an office where you have no contacts and trying to sell them your products). That was my day job.

I pulled out a letter from one of my dear actor friends. She was beautiful, smart, talented, and continuing her studies at a London acting conservatory. I was selling computers by day and doing theatre at night. I was jealous. I wished I could still be safe in school.

That moment stands out in my mind because I was willing to do that difficult and boring job so that I could be an actor. I hated it and didn't want to do it, but I knew it was a means to an end. My acting career wasn't going to be handed to me, and I couldn't afford more school at the time (I had paid for my own college through loans, scholarships, and grants). I had to be willing to make disciplined choices to get me where I wanted to be. I was paying my rent by working the day job that allowed me to do theatre at night. It was all in alignment with my bigger goal of moving to Chicago where I would be able to discover opportunities in a larger acting community.

Dispatches from the Field—Carl

Many of my students stay in touch after graduation. They often seek advice about decisions they need to make. I was having coffee with a recent graduate. He was catching me up on his life after college and told me that he had found a job waiting tables in a popular restaurant. He liked the people who worked there, and he was making good money. He said he had made some good friends and thought it was nice to be out in the "world" creating relationships with people who had experiences other than attending American University. Later in the conversation, I asked him to tell me about his acting career. He told me that his days were busy and that he wasn't accomplishing as much as he had hoped. I thought, here I am listening to a person who took a full load of classes, held down a job, and rehearsed at least one show a semester while he was student. I asked why he wasn't getting anything accomplished if he was only working one job. "By the time I get up, run a few errands, and go to the gym, it's time to get to work," he said. Further investigation revealed that he and his new pals at work were going out after their shifts and staying up into the early morning hours. His day would start around 1:00 or 2:00 in the afternoon. I pointed this out to him, and he said, "I can't just go home and go straight to bed. I'm pretty wound up after a shift." Fair enough. However, staying out until 3:00 in the morning was probably not the only solution to "unwinding" after work. He wasn't minding his edge. The alternative of going home and watching television is not as much fun, but it would have helped him find more time in his day.

Disciplined actors treat time like the precious commodity it is and are disciplined about the allocation of it. As an actor, you will need to put yourself on a schedule that allows you to be awake and alert while the rest of the world is doing business.

Discipline is the place where most actors trip up. They fall short because they make excuses, engage in deceptive self-talk, allow others to discourage them, or are too lazy to roll up their sleeves. To stay one step ahead of the challenges requires tremendous determination.

The plan you devise for advancing your career is about the obvious actions—going on auditions, submitting your headshot and resume to casting directors and agents—and about subtle steps like attending performances, supporting other artists, and contributing to a positive work environment in your day job. The plan will take effort and require delayed gratification. It will involve the discipline it takes to be patient as well as proactive.

Some of the actions you take won't be instantly noticed by anyone, but their repercussions will be felt in the future. We call this doing the "invisible" work—action steps taken when there is no one there telling you what to do or cheering you on. If you are disciplined, you do it anyway. These unglamorous but necessary actions require you to motivate yourself and do tasks like updating your mailing list, taking a dance class, or learning a new monologue. Although the payoff may not be immediate, you will be ready when opportunities arise.

As an actor, you are the CEO of your own company.

There are plenty of reasons for lack of discipline: laziness, fear of failure, fear of success, poor self-esteem, anger, wanting to skip the tough work, wanting someone to do it for you. ("My problems will all be solved when I get an agent.")

Remember—as an actor, you are the CEO of your own company. You are in charge and responsible for your career. You need to care deeply about your career. No one cares more about your career than you do, especially when you are starting out. Once you become more established, you will have more people on your team, helping you accomplish goals. But now, you are at the beginning of the journey; therefore, the hard work, discipline, and commitment is up to you.

Audition for everything, even if you think you're wrong for it. You never know what kind of impression you'll make or who you'll meet. Plus, the more you get into the habit of auditioning, the more relaxed you'll be when you walk into that audition room. Force yourself to go to an audition, even if you're not feeling up to it. Go anyway! I almost talked myself out of going to a particular audition because I procrastinated about learning a new monologue. I forced myself to learn one anyway the night before, went to the audition the next day, and that one production led to twelve straight years of doing *Forever Plaid* all over the country. I never could have predicted that happening, but it might not have happened if I had chosen not to go to the audition because I "didn't feel like it."
— Stephen Wallem, actor

Me and My Disciplined Habits

Exercise: Let's begin by creating a definition. Take three minutes and write your definition of discipline. (Utilize blank pages in the back of the book as necessary.)

What does discipline mean to you?

Now read what you wrote.

What aspects or elements of that definition seem difficult, challenging, or off-putting to you? (Write for another three minutes.)

Now make a list of the things you do regularly that consciously require discipline. For most of us that would not include taking a shower or eating, but it might include exercise, keeping in touch with a friend or family member who lives far away, writing in a journal, etc.

Look at that list. Notice all the ways you are disciplined. Know that you have the capacity to be a disciplined actor. Now that you've created the list, go back and ask yourself why you choose to be disciplined in these particular areas.

Now make a list of disciplined habits you'd like to create.

Ask yourself why you have not already created these habits in your life. Be honest. No one will see this but you. Ask yourself if there is a compelling enough motivation to follow through with the habits.

If there's no motivation to create a particular habit, then you may not really want or need to implement that habit at all. It is important to first understand your current habits before you can move forward.

Keep what you've written thus far. We will examine it further in an upcoming chapter.

Further Reflection . . .

- Were there any surprises on your list of habits to create?
- How would you rate your ability to be disciplined?
- Is there one thing you could change to become more disciplined?

Chapter 4

Disciplined Thought

It's How You Spin It

*Y*ou are involved in a business that is competitive, subjective, and filled with opinionated people.

It is easy to understand why actors might feel insecure. They are frequently turned down for jobs, and can have their art brutally criticized in very public forums. It takes discipline to think positively. As a young actor, now is the time to develop the discipline of removing negative energy from your thoughts and staying focused on your goals of fulfillment and success. You must develop and maintain a "can do" attitude. You need to figure out a strategy for yourself so that you can be undaunted, no matter what comes your way. You must unwaveringly commit to your success in the industry.

If you are really disciplined, then you are auditioning for everything. You go on as many auditions as possible and you network. In spite of your disciplined practices, you will experience rejection. More auditions means more rejection, but it also means improving your chances of being hired. (How many people in other industries could go on several job interviews a day and not allow rejection to undermine their confidence?)

You must be willing to develop a mind-set that doesn't take rejection personally, treats not getting hired as a fact rather than a reflection of your ability and talent, and doesn't allow you to become jaded by the ups and downs caused by the audition cycle. Be aware that it is a process and decide not to let it diminish you. Some salespeople keep themselves motivated by deciding that the current "no" they hear is just bringing them one step closer to the "yes" they are waiting for.

> There are plenty of emotional/psychological traps in the acting biz. Auditions are the #1 opportunity for self-judgment and self-condemnation, second-guessing and overanalyzing. Keep it in perspective. Every audition is not a verdict on your talent, humanity, or worth. We all have to figure out how to be present and powerful in that situation. Prepare for an audition in the way that frees you to let go and be in the moment.
> — Steven Hauck, actor

Ultimately, you can't control the outcome of your auditions, but you can control your actions and self-defeating thoughts. You can't make someone cast you, but you can do your best at an audition. One of Lori's former agents observed, "The happiest actors are those who audition, forget about it, and move on." Decide to make that type of mind-set your goal. Be that kind of actor. It will allow you to ride the roller coaster of your acting career with less emotional wear and tear and more grace and enjoyment. If you need help creating strategies for positive thinking, we've listed some references in the appendix.

The happiest actors are those who audition, forget about it, and move on.

It's important to learn the difference between "I'm not good enough" and "They are looking for someone that is not me." Here's one way to look at it. You've probably heard the expression, "Choose the right tool for the job." If a carpenter is in need of a hammer, a wrench is probably not going to do the job properly. The carpenter could try banging a nail with a wrench, but it'll be a frustrating endeavor. Imagine that a director is looking in the toolbox. If you're the wrench then you won't be used when the director is looking for the hammer. You may say, "I am a hammer, really, I am." And you may be one, but in the world of entertainment, there are many types of hammers a director could choose. It would make no sense to use a tiny hammer for pounding large nails into thick boards. The director has the opportunity to choose, not only the right tool, but the perfect tool for the job. It can be frustrating and seemingly unfair. If you feel hurt, angry, or frustrated often enough, your positive outlook can suffer some serious damage. Know that not every opportunity is meant for you and that part of the process is to constantly seek projects that are right for you. This will help you manage the feelings associated with rejection and steer your thoughts in a more constructive direction.

Being proactive about finding your next job or audition opportunity is a way to take any frustration you may feel and channel it in a positive direction. Start preparing for your next audition. Decide to add a skill to your list of special talents rather than perpetuating the feelings and thoughts that undermine and destroy your self-esteem and, ultimately, your career. Learn to play an instrument. You'd be surprised at how many actors, particularly in musicals, win roles because they are proficient at an instrument. Learn a language. A conversational mastery of French or Spanish can put you that much ahead of another actor. Read the paper, learn to paint, become a photographer, take up knitting, or master juggling. Use your energies to expand your abilities rather than diminish your self-worth.

This is not to say you shouldn't feel disappointed if you don't get cast in a role you wanted or a job you desired. Being disappointed is normal and appropriate. You're human and you're allowed to feel what you feel. Give yourself permission to have a "mourning" period—a time to feel disappointed. This doesn't mean becoming self-indulgent, self-pitying, or polluting the world around you with your anger. (You may find it hard to believe, but some actors are quite dramatic off-stage.) Eventually, you will need to give yourself a break and shut off any internal monologue of self-doubt or bad-mouthing and blaming anyone including yourself, the director, your roommate, your acting teachers, and so on. This may sound easier said than done, but once you decide to become more aware of your negative thinking, the more you will catch yourself when you get into a cycle of destructive thought. When you find yourself going there, you may want to keep in mind a few simple thoughts:

I was well prepared for that audition. I know how to effectively present myself at an audition and I did that.

I did my best at that audition and it's okay to feel disappointed that I didn't get the job.

Don't make these statements if they are not completely true. Be honest with yourself about the audition. Were you as good as you could be? Did you do your homework and prepare to the best of your ability? If you don't have a positive answer to these questions, get to work on the obstacles that impede your ability to audition well. Did you appear overly nervous? Learning to mange nervousness is something all actors must handle and overcome—particularly when they are first auditioning. Take an audition class. Read books that discuss techniques for successful auditioning. We've listed a few in the appendix. If you haven't mastered audition techniques, then you won't get very far in this business.

To get work you must develop and maintain your talents and skills. The skills you acquired in college or in your classes may need to be sharper when you compete against more experienced actors. Invest in dance, voice, and acting lessons, even when you're working. Don't let "I don't have the money" stop you. If you really believe in your talent and believe you *have* to do this with your life, then you have to invest in it. The best artists are life-long learners who recognize that skills not only need to be developed, but kept *sharp*.

> Pretty people have an easier time in this business than "ordinary" people. It's a fact of our profession and it often seems unfair, but there's not a damn thing you can do about it. If you're one of the beautiful people, consider yourself blessed. If you're not, you'll have to work harder—and taking care of your appearance matters. Weight matters; fitness matters; being comfortable in your skin and happy with your looks matters.
> — Mark Ramont, director

> Never, ever get caught up in the cliché that you have to be "beautiful" to make it in this business. Trust me, character actors often have much longer careers, and if you do happen to be a beautiful leading man or leading lady-type, make sure you are just as adept at character work so you can still get work after your good looks no longer have the same magic!
> — Stephen Wallem, actor

After you've considered your *personal success* at the audition (we mean how well you auditioned, not whether or not you got cast), move forward by saying two things.

They were looking for something different.

It was someone else's turn and mine is coming.

If you don't think you can remember these statements or if you think you'll forget to use them, make them easily accessible. Laminate them on a small card that you keep in your bag or wallet. Post them in obvious places in your room or apartment. Make them the screen saver or background on your computer. Having these phrases in your arsenal of positive thought will be an active step in maintaining an appropriate perspective. It may take a while before these become mantras. You may have to say them after many auditions before they become second nature and part of your thought process, but eventually, you will take control over something that is within your control—your ability to provide yourself with an informed, honest assessment of your work.

You may also encounter situations when it seems as though it is always *someone else's* turn. These times are particularly difficult when that someone else—a friend, roommate, or someone in your social circle—skyrockets to a success that seems out of reach to you. Often these situations provoke feelings of envy. Perhaps you blame the director, the other actor, or even worse, you go into a spiral of feeling inadequate. Obviously, these thoughts and feelings will not lead to a positive outcome. Rather than dwelling in a negative place, try to consider the steps you can take to achieve success. Focus on moving forward. Ask yourself, "What is that other person doing that I'm not?"

You also have to consider the fact that many actors don't get their break for years. Sometimes they need to grow into their type. Your type might be the wise old confidant who advises the hero about love, but you're not going to get those roles until you're old enough to play them. Be sure not to consider that an excuse for sitting back and waiting for your "time" to arrive.

It can be difficult to work hard when you feel like you have "nothing to show for it." Going on lots of auditions without booking a job or even getting a callback can be tremendously discouraging. It's important to remember that you are not doing "all of this work for nothing." Your efforts aren't pointless. Here's a perspective that might help you steer clear of feelings of futility.

Imagine that you decide to construct a new house. You pour a foundation, build a frame, install the interior and exterior walls, etc. Every day you go to the construction site and work hard. Every day you build that house, but at the end of the day you can't live there. Even though the house is yours, you may not feel like it is. On top of the time it takes to build your house, there often are unforeseen set-backs: a lumber order doesn't get delivered; the subcontractor installs the wrong tile and it has to be ripped out and re-installed. These delays may slow down the process. Construction of a new home seldom adheres to the predetermined completion date, but eventually the house is built and you move in. Once you do, then you have to paint, decorate, install blinds, landscape the yard (and the list goes on).

Show up every day at the construction site called your career. Understand that construction won't always go as planned. Expect the unanticipated holdups and slowdowns, but remember that *you still own the house.* You will eventually reside there, renovate it, build an addition, replace the roof, install a sound system—get the idea?

There is no such thing as wasted energy if the effort is focused on constructively advancing your career. Arm yourself with that thought.

Dispatches from the Field—Lori

Early in my career, I got so upset and disappointed when I didn't get cast in a role that at times I would stay in bed for a day and cry. I know it sounds dramatic, but I felt personally wounded by the rejection, and to cope, I would immerse myself in negative, unproductive feelings. I called it "sliding into the sewer." It seemed impossible that there would ever be another opportunity. However, when the next audition presented itself, I would start to climb back out of the sewer, pull myself together, and show up for the audition. It was a lot of work to continually go up and down on that emotional roller coaster. Out of self-preservation, I finally realized I couldn't keep going on like that. It was too much work!

What I see now that I couldn't see then is that I allowed thoughts about my self-worth to be contingent on someone hiring me. Not getting the job defined the way I felt about myself and who I was as a person. Sometimes it hurts when I don't get a role I want, but luckily, my self-esteem is much higher and I am no longer devastated by not getting the job. Generally, I try to focus my attention away from myself and onto helping others when I am disappointed. Being of service to others—acting as a sounding board to friends and colleagues, supporting people who are in need, or mentoring young actors—helps me feel better about myself. These positive actions lead directly to positive thinking. When I'm successful in shifting my thinking, I feel hopeful and back on track so much faster.

Dispatches from the Field—Carl

Several years ago, a talented young man came to the university as a freshman theatre major. During his first semester, he was cast in a production and given a significant role. His performance was impressive. Not only was he an incredibly talented actor but he was a thoughtful, respectful person. At the beginning of his second semester, he was called back for a principal role in a main stage production. He was not cast. Days later, he came to my office and asked if he could talk to me about the auditions. I was not directing the show so I wasn't sure what information he wanted from me—I was unable to give him feedback about his audition. After beating around the bush for a few minutes, he confessed that he was upset with himself because he was feeling jealous of the actor who was cast in the role he wanted. He was struggling with his negative feelings and said he didn't want to turn his disappointment into jealousy. I was astonished that he was this self-aware. I told him that we have no control over what we feel, but we can control what we do with those feelings. The other actor had something my student wanted, and his first reaction was to feel jealous. You feel what you feel and no one should tell you to feel differently. I praised him for his honesty and asked that he allow himself to be disappointed but not turn that disappointment into destructive thought, behavior, or words. It was amazing how reassuring these words were to him. He just needed to know that it was okay to feel what he felt.

It's when that jealousy spirals into destructive thought that people get in trouble. If my student began to criticize the other actor, the director, or himself for not being any good or not knowing what they were doing or doubting their capabilities then he would have been on a slippery slope of self-destruction. Separating our feelings about the situation versus dwelling on misdirected feeling toward others is a great way to exercise disciplined thought.

Self-awareness is so critical in the process of warding off negative thought. See if you can notice the pattern. When does negative self-talk start to show up for you? Do certain kinds of situations trigger it? Connect to your reason for it. Become aware of how the process happens for you. Once you become more aware of the times when negative self-talk begins, try to "head it off at the pass" simply by saying *stop*. Try to take a moment; become aware of your breathing. Give yourself permission to have the feelings that bring about the negative self-talk, but put an end to that negative internal monologue. Do something else. Take a walk. Work out or talk to a trusted friend. Make yourself feel better by doing something positive for someone else. Deal with the feelings and avoid the negative criticism of yourself and others. Redirect your thinking. When you raise your awareness and begin to tame the wild beast called negative self-talk, the negativity will cease to consume your thinking and give you the choice to take a more positive path.

Disciplined thought is all about MTE. Avoiding the urge to dwell on negative thought means you remain positive. That positive approach will translate into outward actions that keep you moving forward. Developing self-awareness is vital to your success. Issues regarding negative, self-sabotaging thoughts and actions are extremely complex. If you spend too much time in a swirl of negative thinking, it's time to seek professional assistance.

Your Audition Logbook

Exercise: **This tool will help you have a more balanced and informed perspective about your job search and serve as a record to reference for future auditions.**

Create a computer file or purchase a blank journal that you can devote entirely to auditions. After each audition write the following:

- *The name of the production, show, film, commercial, etc.*

- *The name of the agent, casting director, or director*
  Each audition will have a separate page and you will continue to record your auditions and track your progress with the particular individual.

- *What you wore, what you sang, and/or the scenes you performed*

- *All the positive things you did at the audition*
  For example, I was on time; I was well prepared; I felt good about myself and how I presented myself; etc.

- *Anything you wish you would have done differently*
  For example, next time I will research the director's previous work; I will make stronger choices; etc.
- *Notes about your interactions with the auditors*
  What was their response to you/your audition?
  Things you'd like to remember about them for future auditions
  Any personal exchange you may have had
  Suggestions for your future auditions
- *Notes about your callbacks*

As you keep a record of your auditions, you will begin to see patterns and improvements. By consciously reflecting on each audition, you will take control of things you can control. You will also be able to reference your audition logbook when a director or casting director you auditioned for previously calls you in for a different project. When that happens, you can go back and read what you wrote. You may discover useful information that helps you prepare for your future auditions.

As an actor, you need to be your biggest fan. Examine how you think about yourself and your circumstances and then determine what you can control. Find ways to process and cope with what is out of your control. You are the only one inside your head, so be disciplined in your thinking. Learn to silence your negative, disapproving internal voice. Focus on positive and empowering thoughts. Take concrete actions that make those thoughts reality. Do all that you can to keep yourself vibrant, buoyed, and available for the next opportunity.

Chapter 5

Invasion of the Neg-a-Tors

Rising above Negativity

*H*ere's a new word, "neg-a-tor." We made it up and we definitely made up the B-movie title for this chapter. Neg-a-tors are the external negative forces, people, thoughts, and opinions that bring us down. How you respond to neg-a-tors is up to you.

No one likes to be around negative people. Do you enjoy listening to people complain? Do you enjoy listening to people talk trash? Do you ever worry that you might be the subject of that trash talk when you're not around? People sometimes feel that if they diminish the work of others, they will gain in stature or status. In truth, all they gain is a reputation for being nasty.

Aren't complainers fun!? You too can be a neg-a-tor! It's easy, and once you start, you could probably convince those around you to join in, and suddenly there will be an "invasion of neg-a-tors." How many times have you seen a production or film and afterward engaged in a lengthy bad-mouthing session of the work? Come on, admit it. Ask yourself how many of the potshots you made came from your jealousy or insecurity? What makes you think that anyone enjoys listening to you gripe and complain? Are your complaints somehow more legitimate than others? Remember that when you do it, you have the same effect that others have on you when they complain.

Sometimes, it seems easier to be negative than it is to be positive. Being positive requires that you think before you speak. It requires that you take the high road. It requires that you rise above the pettiness that might surround you. It requires discipline. It requires you to be the bigger person. Don't you admire and respect people who choose not to negatively engage with the world? They somehow seem above the fray. But remember, it's a *choice* they make—the *choice* to positively engage with others.

Celebrate good work—even if it's not your own. If everything sucks then the future of the American theatre or the entertainment industry itself is in jeopardy. Therefore, your career would be in serious jeopardy as well. There is plenty of bad work out in the world. It gets produced for all kinds of reasons. Make sure you know the difference between your own jealousy and insecurity and your ability to spot weak art. There's ample room for everyone to be wonderful. Take a step back for a moment and find other ways to respond to work. It's fine to acknowledge that something was not well done, but once you do that, leave it alone. Spouting off about someone's bad performance or spending an entire postshow evening ranting about it will accomplish nothing in the end. Don't lead the charge of negativity, especially not in a professional situation. It's very unprofessional to listen to actors on break at rehearsal get worked up and nasty about another professional. Zip it!

Don't you admire and respect people who choose not to negatively engage with the world? They somehow seem above the fray. But remember, it's a choice they make—the choice *to be positive.*

Challenge yourself to find something positive to say. We don't mean that you need to be a Pollyanna. People can be upbeat without being irritating. But you need to control the urge to plunge into the pool of negativity. Does it really make you feel better? Does it accomplish anything (other than make you look negative and petty)? It only adds to the bitterness that so frequently permeates the world of show business.

Your profession and your city (as large as it may seem) are small. While there may be lots of actors doing what you do; it doesn't take long for people to get to know who's who. It also doesn't take long for word to get around if you are negative and difficult. On the other hand, it doesn't take long for people to realize that you contribute something positive to a process.

It is a huge challenge to behave professionally and positively when the situation around you is negative or people behave unprofessionally. Avoid the urge to have the neg-a-tors take over. Be part of the solution and not the problem.

Dispatches from the Field—Lori

Years ago, I auditioned for a fun-sounding musical comedy, but the job was several hours from where I lived at the time and I wasn't really interested in commuting. I'll admit I had a bit of an attitude as I drove the long drive to the audition. After auditioning with the sides and songs they provided, they asked me to improvise a scene. To my surprise and horror, I ended up being outrageously angry in the improv to the point of picking up a chair and throwing it madly on the stage. I had some rage that wasn't in check. After the audition (and can you imagine—I didn't get the job!) I was really upset and blamed them for my feelings of embarrassment, acting as if they had made me behave that way. In truth, I had let my negativity control me, and I wasn't being honest with myself about going out for jobs I didn't want.

A friend of mine got the job and played opposite a wonderful actor who eventually became her husband. They are happily married and have a family. I was not meant to get that job—it was her job. Looking back, I can see how everything worked out perfectly. It was a great wake-up call for me to work through and acquire the necessary skills to be in charge of actions that come from my emotions.

Dispatches from the Field—Carl

When I was a young teacher, I taught in a New England prep school. One of my colleagues had been there more than thirty years. He and I had a good relationship, but I was always aware that he viewed me as a "kid." (I was in my late twenties.) We worked well together, but I often disagreed with his educational philosophy. He had a reputation for complaining about the school and the headmaster to anyone who would listen. It always seemed as though he was recruiting people to join his chorus of "neg-a-tors." (I often wondered why he didn't find another job if conditions at the school were so terrible.) A few years into my tenure at the job, I sat next to him in a meeting and voiced my opinion regarding a group of students who were suspended and faced expulsion. I thought the situation surrounding the suspension needed further investigation before we enforced such a serious consequence. He summarily dismissed this group of students as troublemakers. I told him I thought we needed to understand the situation from the students' point of view. He answered by saying, "This kind of thing has been going on since I began teaching. Kids don't change." "But the world around them does," I replied. He dismissed me and led the charge to permanently remove the students. I looked at him in that moment and thought, "When I'm fifty-something, I will not be like this cynical man who can't listen or consider perspectives other than my own."

Fast forward to my next teaching job, where I taught for many years in a suburban school system outside of Chicago. I was a committed teacher and a hard worker. I ran a theatre program for almost ten years. The job entailed long hours and late nights (producing high school plays can be a giant challenge). I made a deliberate point to avoid the neg-a-tors.

One day, I passed a colleague in the hall who asked how I was. I responded that I was "great, thank you." He stopped and said. "Don't you ever have a bad day? Don't things ever go wrong? Doesn't this place ever get on your nerves?" I looked at him and responded, "Dwelling on that is far too depressing." He avoided me after that. Sure, there were things about that job that got me down, but I knew my audience and voiced my disappointments in an appropriate place and time. Bitching about the school in the hallways where students might hear was not exactly the example I wanted to set. I waited to express strong opinions and feelings when I was with close friends and colleagues in a setting where my comments would be viewed as venting my frustration rather than complaining. There are appropriate venues to voice our complaints, gripes, and dissatisfaction, but make sure you do it with people who will not repeat your words out of context or share them with others you don't trust. Choose your audience wisely.

While all of these things seem obvious, they require a deliberate effort on your part. You have to make the conscious commitment to being a positive professional. (Even if you feel negative and nasty inside—fake it. After a while, you may find that "faking it" is a habit that becomes a genuine attitude.) Some days you will be better at it than others. When you're not a positive influence or you bring negative energy to the workplace, take the time to remind yourself exactly how you would like to behave. Once you've reflected on the situation, move on with a commitment to improve. Everyone has an occasional bad day. You don't need to dwell on it. Just make sure that the occasional bad day doesn't become the norm for you.

Hunting for Neg-a-Tors

Exercise: **Choose a work or social event that involves at least four or more people engaged in a single conversation. It can be a rehearsal, a party, or just hanging out with a group of friends.**

Once you see that the group has "warmed up" keep mental track of the negative and the positive comments. Observe the following:

- How do people generally respond to negative comments?
- What were their nonverbal reactions?
- What was their tone of voice?
- Do you find that certain people tend to make negative or positive comments?
- How do people respond to the negative people in general?

We know that you can assume the answers, but it's more important to notice specific behaviors, and reactions. Once you raise your awareness about other people's negative behavior you may discover that it's much easier to keep yours in check.

Further Reflection . . .

- **Did the "neg-a-tors" you identified in the above exercise gravitate toward a particular theme?**
- **How did you resist the urge to jump on board?**

- How did you respond in that setting?
- Can you take a guess as to what may have been behind the negativity?

Dispatches from the Field—Lori

As an eager young actor, I signed up for an on-camera acting class at a prestigious studio in Chicago. The instructor was one of the top-notch teachers in town, and I was really excited to learn from her. On the first day of class, she walked into the room and said, "I know you all hate yourselves." I was floored. I knew that I was struggling with self-esteem, but for her to view us as self-loathing students seemed an inappropriate power trip designed to "break us down." She never offered us solutions for building self-esteem, but she was really good at tearing us down in class. At the time, I didn't have the courage to drop the class. I know now that taking care of myself is imperative and that just because someone is an authority or expert doesn't make him or her right. I now use my instincts to determine if something is right for me—especially when I'm paying for the experience or class.

In this business, the last thing we need is an environment where toxic people actively attempt to destroy our confidence, self-worth, and personal power.

Keeping Your Neg-a-Tor at Bay

Exercise: **Sometimes we are in situations we can't control and are forced to be with neg-a-tors.**

Write down one work- or school-related issue that is frequently the subject of group complaining. Example: a professor or student who is not liked by others.

Spend a few minutes writing down all the reasons why people complain. (Utilize blank pages in the back of the book as necessary.)

Think of everything positive there is to say on the subject—even if it seems small and insignificant. There's usually something positive to say about a subject. Now, use that list to come up with a polite, positive, diplomatic way to respond when the subject is raised by a fellow student.

Make a conscious effort to avoid conversation around the topic, and when it is unavoidable choose to deal with it positively or not at all. You don't have to scold your peers, you just have to choose not to engage (there's a huge difference). No one wants to work with someone who is "holier than thou."

You can employ this strategy of finding a positive comment in any situation where you see people complaining about the topic de jour.

Further Reflection . . .
- **How effective was your strategy for finding positive comments and avoiding your inner "neg-a-tor"?**
- **How did your peers respond?**
- **Were you surprised by any reactions (yours or theirs)?**

It's important to remember that silence is power. Once you spill your guts, you have to own your comments because they came out of your mouth. You also make yourself vulnerable to comments by others. Sometimes it's impossible to avoid negative situations or make a positive comment. Often, the most powerful response is no response.

Sometimes it's impossible to avoid negative situations or make a positive comment. Often, the most powerful response is no response.

There are powerful lessons to be learned from working in toxic situations. They may not be enjoyable, but they can teach us about how we want to interact professionally. Find what is valuable in those situations. Perhaps you've heard the expression, "take what you need and leave the rest." There are lessons to be learned in every situation. Discipline yourself to look for them.

> . . . just keep practicing and honing your craft. Don't turn down an opportunity to work; it doesn't matter where or what the role is. It's very true that "there are no small roles . . . only small actors." Every acting experience comes with some education; whether it's knowing how to work with a star, working with a particular director, choreographer, designer, or producer—or doing a role you thought was nothing like any you imagined yourself doing. Just do it. Angela Lansbury didn't become Angela Lansbury by turning down the offer to play a maid or someone's mother.
> — Barry Brown, producer

Chapter 6

Disciplined Action

Follow-Through

> Hard work will win out over talent every time. I've seen
> mediocre talents rise to the top because they are driven to
> succeed; and I've seen amazingly talented people fall by the
> wayside because they aren't able to find a way to consistently give
> their all. You can't do anything about talent (or lack of) except
> work hard to develop it to its fullest potential. God-given talent
> is only potential that will come to nothing without hard work.
> — Mark Ramont, director

*M*any successful actors will tell you that it took hard work to develop
the disciplined habits that led to their success. While many actors have
the desire to be more disciplined, closer investigation will reveal that
the *successful* actors are those who can translate that desire into action.

The only way to create a disciplined habit is to have the motivation and the drive to do so. As much as you might wish you had more
audition monologues, you will never learn new ones if you aren't
burning to get ahead in "the business." One of the ways to develop a
habit is to start small. One reason people avoid acquiring a habit is the
fact that they view the task and the effort as monumental. Instead of

dividing the task into small doable pieces, they feel so overwhelmed by the entirety of the job that they never begin it. In the end, they deprive themselves of the opportunity to move forward and develop that new habit. They trap themselves in a world of good intentions and, eventually, fall over the edge and into free fall of procrastination and excuse-making.

Here's a simple way to develop a habit. "Piggyback" the new task onto an existing part of your routine. Begin by making the task manageable (keep it the right size). Doing this will keep that task out of the range of the procrastination mind game. Have patience with yourself. You can't run a marathon until you can run a half-mile first. Remember that the goal is progress, not perfection. Here's an exercise to put you on the path to a disciplined habit:

Identifying and Creating Disciplined Habits

Exercise: **Take a few minutes and answer these questions:**

1. *What are the tasks you do on a daily basis? (Brushing your teeth, checking your e-mail, washing the breakfast dishes, etc.)*

2. *What are your weekly and daily tasks that require discipline? (Calling parents once a week, going to yoga, doing laundry, etc.)*

3. *What are the tasks that you do sporadically that you wish you did more often? (Going to the gym, reading scripts, keeping a journal, etc.)*

4. *Why don't you regularly commit to the activities you listed in question 3? (Too tired, no time, don't feel like it, something came up)*

5. *Why do you regularly commit to the tasks you listed in questions 1 and 2? (My teeth would rot, I want to stay fit, I don't want my apartment to have a roach problem)*

You will find that the tasks on the first two lists are important if not essential to you—so much so, that you make the effort to perform them regularly.

Go back and look at the list of habits you created in the exercise on disciplined habits on pp. 59–60.

Choose one task from that list. Ask yourself, "Why don't I do this?" For example, "I wish I were more disciplined about sending out postcards to agents and casting directors. I don't do it because it is boring, and to do it right I'd have to send out fifty postcards a week."

Reduce this task to something manageable:

"I will send out five postcards to the most important contacts this week."

Determine a time when you can do this on a regular basis and "piggyback" the task to an existing task.

"Every Thursday I watch a certain TV show. I will take ten minutes before I watch the show and write five postcards."

Commit to writing five postcards for ten minutes on Thursdays. Treat it like a regular appointment. Enter it on your calendar. Acknowledge your accomplishment of the task—or perhaps, give yourself a star.

Once you complete this task for four consecutive Thursdays, begin to increase the number of postcards:

"I will send out seven postcards on Thursdays and Sundays before I watch my favorite shows."

Acknowledge that you are moving in a positive direction. Celebrate having *done the job*—not the results.

You know yourself and know what is and isn't manageable. You know the point at which you'll start that mind game of putting off the habit. Keep the task well out of the range of that mind game.

Further Reflection . . .

- **How long did it take to develop a new habit?**
- **In what ways were you successful in creating a new habit?**
- **What were the impediments to creating the habit?**
- **What strategy did you use to develop your habit?**

Dispatches from the Field—Carl

Okay, this one's not from the classroom but it's a good example of developing a habit. Not long ago, a good friend of mine was serving overseas in the military. We e-mailed and spoke on the phone occasionally. Once, I asked him if he wanted me to tell him about life in DC or if that would make him feel homesick. He said that even though it did make him feel homesick the newsy e-mails from home made him feel connected and not so far away. I made up my mind to send him a daily e-mail. Finding a time to do this was a challenge. What I decided to do was piggyback my new habit to an existing one. It is my morning ritual to sit with a cup of coffee and read the paper. I made up my mind that before I opened the paper, I would send my daily e-mail to my friend. I carved a place into an existing routine to create a new one. When he came home from overseas a year later, it took me a while to realize that I didn't have to start my day at the computer writing an e-mail. In a short time I had developed an ingrained habit.

Dispatches from the Field—Lori

I have to say that I have different levels of disciplined action. There are some tasks that I have been doing since I started as an actor and have no resistance to doing them. I really enjoy sending out mailings, headshots, and resumes and meeting new people. My father is a fantastic salesman and role model when it comes to his business. I am always inspired by the joy he takes in his work and the pleasure he brings to others. He always shows up with a good attitude and a willingness to work hard.

In the areas of "the business" where discipline hasn't come easily to me, I find that seeking assistance from trusted peers is invaluable. They understand me and "the business" and are willing to help me move forward. I use a simple, yet highly effective tool I learned called "bookending." It's a great way to accomplish something I have a hard time doing. I call up a trusted friend and tell her that I need some support to take action on a task I am resistant to complete. For example, I tend to procrastinate when it comes to rehearsing music or lines on my own. I tell the friend exactly what I need to accomplish and ask if I can call her back or text when I have completed the dreaded task. If I don't contact her, I have to acknowledge the fact that a good friend or colleague knows I made a commitment to do something and didn't follow through. What's great about this type of support is that I don't have to feel as though I am alone on the project. It's also not a big commitment for the friend. It actually builds trust with my friend because now she can feel comfortable "bookending" with me. It's a win-win situation because it creates accountability, and gets the tasks done!

Disciplined actions and follow-through are the keys to building career momentum. Identify your personal brand of resistance when it comes to taking certain actions. *Recognize the distractions and excuses that sidetrack you. Then ask yourself if you have a determined, unwavering commitment to fulfillment and success. If so, then you will find a way to push past your resistance, distractions and excuses.* Set yourself up for success. Present yourself with manageable tasks. Seek support if you need encouragement. Remember to celebrate even the smallest accomplishment or forward movement. Do this until the task is either completed or becomes part of your routine.

Chapter 7

The 80-Year Plan

When Timelines become "Dead Lines"

Of course it is human nature to make plans—to actively *work* toward some goal and perhaps see it achieved rather than passively waiting, say for the next message from our agent, if we have one. But in that dreamland actors call The Big Time, we all, at one time or another, invest in a kind of Time Share. It is often called a goal. An excellent goal is to be *ready* for what *really* happens when it happens, not only for what we *wish* would happen right now! Frequently, both are quite different. We do not control the quixotic whims of the theatre gods. So, like going to the gym, we need to keep stretching and developing our acting muscles to make us ready and able to handle the demands of the job whenever it appears.

But should these goals be *scheduled* to happen by a certain age? If they are, they are often wisely replaced along the way. Making goals too structured and rigid leaves little room for those suddenly appearing *better* possibilities that can and *do* flash across our paths, like a meteor, and move us unexpectedly higher. A career's timelines are similar to a moving escalator whose distant top is often obscured in the fog of reality. We get on the escalator, so why not enjoy the ride? We are not empowered to see into the future.
— Bill Yule, actor/writer, age 82

Some actors are driven by age-related timelines: "By the time I'm 30 I will [fill in the blank]." What happens if today's goal to be on Broadway by age 30 isn't met as you blow out your 30 birthday candles? Does that make you a failure? Should you throw your tap shoes out the window? Do you give up at age 30 because what you think should have happened didn't? Obviously, we know the answer to that question, but we're trying to illustrate how ridiculous some timelines can be. Some goals need timelines, but often, age-driven timelines are arbitrary and based on assumptions and external influences. Why should we have a definition of what success looks like at a specific age? How would it feel to reframe your dream by saying, "I'm not in a Broadway show *yet*?" Sometimes timelines are appropriate for setting goals—"I will learn a new audition monologue this month"—and sometimes they are arbitrary markers for success based on a misunderstood notion of longevity and vitality.

While a timeline will certainly help you focus and put your goals in a context, don't use it as an excuse to be a failure and quit. Don't let a randomly chosen timeline sabotage you. Some roles in plays or film are age related, but fulfillment doesn't have to be.

Timelines can be external measures of success but not necessarily the keys to fulfillment. Consider the young hotshots that soar right to the top right after college. Very quickly, they are "livin' the dream." Some of them end up stuck in a youthful definition of themselves and don't transform that early success into career longevity. They end up waiting for something to happen instead of actively redefining themselves.

We've decided we're on the 80-year plan. We plan to live until we're 80 and determine at that point how it's going and what else we want to accomplish. We'll see what is aching and creaking and how much fun we're having. Your goals and timelines are chosen by you, so why not extend the idea of how much time you've got to get everything done?

Switch to the 80-year plan. It really feels better than having to get it all done by the time you're 25, 30, or 40. Yes, it is important to know what you want and to pursue goals, but the 80-year plan allows you to continually update and redefine those goals as your life evolves. If you are experiencing your personal fulfillment needs (PFNs), why impose a hard and fast timeline?

While we recognize that there are certain age-related casting realities (you probably won't play Maria in *West Side Story* when you're 65), the 80-year plan means you allow for an ever-evolving sense of your-

Something I've carried with me all these years, that I've learned from observation, is that the need to obtain your goals must be great; that you should truly put forth your whole self into achieving personal success. However, and this is the lesson, it should not be so all-consuming that, if the goal is not fully reached (let's say, the Broadway stage), one should fall into a pit of despair. I have known people who lost their "glow," their spirit, after realizing that who they thought they would become would not transpire; I have seen actors who formerly were bright, happy beings, become bitter, envious, and consumed by what they saw as their "failure." Success comes in many different forms, and one must take stock in personal achievements and ask oneself (as I do regularly), "But have I had fun? Has it been a joy, every time I've had the chance to entertain an audience? Did I love what I was doing? . . . And did I love this life, onstage and off?" For me, yes, and I continue to do so, whether Broadway enters that grand picture or not.
— Bill Selby, actor/director

self as an artist instead of being constrained by arbitrary timelines. So, why not give yourself some time? Stop putting all of your goals in a restrictive time frame. Learn to be flexible. Allow for the fact that there will be surprises and exciting opportunities that are not part of the "plan." Stay open to possibilities you never considered.

By embracing the idea of having many years to fulfill your goals, you can choose to be more accepting of your current circumstances and make wiser decisions because you're taking the long view. Perhaps this will make you more relaxed and willing to take risks. Be audacious! Challenge yourself and dream bigger—don't limit yourself. Take in a deep breath and relax. You have more time than you think.

Chapter 8

Focus Your Actions

Being of Service

WHAT DOES IT MEAN TO BE "OF SERVICE"?

*Y*ou are most likely already being of service in some aspect of your life. You support your friends and/or family members. You donate time or money to charity or a friend in need. You hold a door or let someone get ahead of you in line. There are lots of simple ways in which we are of service in our everyday lives. There is a quote, attributed to Winston Churchill, "We make a living by what we do, we make a life by what we give." It's how you think about it, the mind-set you have, that allows you to see your work as serving others. We believe that being of service will lead to a fulfilling life.

Think about a morning trip to an audition or a class. You'll see lots of people being of service. The person at the local coffee shop helps hundreds of people jump-start their morning. The subway conductor and the bus driver get people where they need to go and help reduce the number of cars on the road. The person who sells you a paper or magazine contributes to the enjoyment of the early part of your day. A security guard keeps the lunatic fringe from entering the building and will keep order in an emergency. A receptionist acts as a gatekeeper, so that others can get their work done more productively and efficiently without interruption . . . get the picture? This may seem incredibly simplistic, but this perspective will help shift your mind-set to one that keeps you positively anchored in the real world. Thinking this way reminds us that no one is more important than anyone else and that we all contribute to the whole.

Being of Service

Exercise: **Respond to each question.**

Describe a time when you were of service to someone or others.

How did you feel during or right after that time? What was the reward?

Have any of those feelings occurred when you have successfully completed an acting project?

Describe an artistic or acting moment when you felt you were of service. What were you feeling?

In their purest form, theatre, television, music, and film fulfill an important role in our culture. At the highest level, artistic expressions:

- Educate
- Entertain
- Enlighten
- Illuminate
- Inspire
- Challenge

To paraphrase Shakespeare, artists hold a mirror up to humanity. Isn't that a service? While this concept may more easily apply to theatre and films that are provocative, pose difficult questions, examine complex topics, or spotlight societal issues that seem marginalized, it might be difficult to defend the notion that doing a commercial about computer software or performing on a cruise ship is "being of service." It's a simple matter of perspective. Sure, you can think that you're prostituting yourself for the benefit of corporate America, or doing uninspired song-and-dance drivel for drunken passengers on a ship. You could also take the perspective that you're exposing consumers to a valuable, time-saving method of dealing with their stressful lives or bringing joy to people who have saved their hard-earned money for a week in the Caribbean. Perhaps this is idealistic, but wouldn't it feel better knowing that you're working for a purpose that's greater than your own checkbook? Again, we're talking about a mindset that you *choose* to adopt. Maybe you've never looked at it this way. You have the choice to approach your work from a variety of perspectives. We're making a suggestion and perhaps opening you to a different way of thinking.

When you share your gifts, you are being of service because your talents enrich the world of those around you. Being of service means you are helpful and provide others with assistance. Some people say that actors are the most selfish people in the world because they are so centered on themselves. Yes, there are selfish actors out there, but no more so than in any other profession. By its nature, being of service, takes us out of ourselves and increases our awareness of others and the world around us. This not only makes us feel better about ourselves, but it also gives us perspective and energy that we might not otherwise attain. When you feel good about yourself you can feel energized, and you can use that positive energy to fuel and inform your creative endeavors, your auditions, and other aspects of your work and life.

A Service Industry

Exercise: **Take three minutes to respond to the questions below. (Utilize blank pages in the back of the book as necessary.)**

In what ways is the entertainment industry a service industry?

Further Reflection . . .

- **Did any of your answers surprise you? If so, how?**
- **Did the exercise reveal anything you hadn't considered? If so, what?**

It's a pretty simple concept. We think you may want to incorporate it.

Once you decide that you're going to be of service, your path becomes positive. Positive does not mean without setbacks or disappointments, but the drive behind your work is infinitely more constructive. Being of service allows you to get out of your own way, and to put vanity and selfishness in check. As you implement the concept of being of service, you will bring positive energy to projects and naturally gravitate toward like-minded colleagues. Developing these attitudes and relationships will serve you well as you go through the ups and downs of your career. Let's further explore what it means to be of service as an actor.

Dispatches from the Field—Lori

Some years ago, a friend introduced me to her grandfather, a successful, accomplished doctor in his 80s. I was inspired by him to make the commitment to being of service. He and I sat in his garden one afternoon while my friend visited with her grandmother. I was taken by his kindness and his positive attitude about life. His contentment was palpable. I asked him why he felt that way, and he told me it was because he felt he had lived and continued to live a gratifying life. I asked him if he would share his recipe for living a meaningful life.

He said the greatest fulfillment in his life came from collaboration with his colleagues and his interactions with patients. The collaboration was energizing, and the joy he got from trying to make his patients feel healthy, reassured, and hopeful was enormously gratifying. I was truly inspired by having met a successful person who was grateful for the gifts his career granted him. I knew he continued to make people feel better, because I felt lighter and happier after I spoke with him. He had been of service for so many years and still brought that energy to his interactions. I tell this story because I realized that everyone has the choice to commit to a career of service. You may be thinking, "It's easy for a doctor and a research scientist to be of service. How does this philosophy translate to my *career as an actor?" The doctor inspired me to commit my acting career to the service of others. Here's an example of how I view my work as service.*

Shortly after meeting him I began to ask myself, "How can I be of service?" Of course, there were the obvious ways—volunteering my time to entertain the elderly at a nursing home or lending my talents to raise money and awareness for a charitable organization. But what about in the way I live my life and create my art?

I have often heard actors talk as though the audience had a greater responsibility than showing up for the performance. One night in the dressing room, an actress said, "It's going to be a small house, I'm not going to put on my eyelashes. They don't deserve it." I was shocked by her attitude. I've always found it unacceptable when I hear a fellow actor say, "What a terrible audience!" because that audience wasn't giv-

ing enough. The truth is that the audience has already done its job—audience members bought their tickets and are sitting in the seats. No matter how many people come to see the show, it is your job to give your best performance. The audience doesn't owe you its laughter or response. People paid their money. They have a right to expect you to deliver the goods. That's one reason why I believe that show business is a "service industry."

I discovered something even more wonderful when I did Mamma Mia! *on Broadway and on the road. It is a "feel-good" musical that I came to think of as the "Joy Factory." I'll never forget the night I saw an elderly man in one of the front rows dancing with his walker-type cane during the big dance finale. He was holding on to the back of the theatre seat in front of him and waving his cane high in the air above his head, swaying to the beat of the music. It was thrilling to see him affected in that way. I looked at him and told myself that I must never forget how this show moves people.*

This was reinforced for me when an associate choreographer flew in from London and called a rehearsal. She asked us to think about the family of four that comes to see a Broadway show and to consider the expenditure of money for an evening's entertainment—$100 per ticket, parking, dinner, and a souvenir program. She told us never to lose sight of the fact that it is our responsibility to make it a special evening for that family. For many, it will be their first Broadway show. It should be nothing short of magical. My experience with the "Joy Factory" gave me tremendous insights and taught me invaluable lessons—every audience deserves my best work; every night is opening night for an audience; I have the ability to positively affect theatre-goers and be part of the magic of the theatre. Since then, it's been easy to see how I can choose to be of service.

Chapter 9

You at Work

> Bring your best self into the room. — Matt Lenz, director

> Be consistent, professional, kind, and work harder than everyone else around you. Learn from and work with those you consider the best in the field. Be humble and honor the people who came before you. Encourage your colleagues!
> — Michael Baron, artistic director/director

*T*hink of a director of a film, play, or TV show as someone preparing to lead an expedition to the top of Mt. Everest. Before starting the expedition, this leader would choose the most knowledgeable, disciplined, and skilled members for her trek team. The team works cooperatively and relies on each member to achieve success. It is imperative for the team to work collaboratively and harmoniously under all types of conditions, especially when the going gets tough. The leader would expect each member of the team to participate fully in the success of the endeavor. You can't have a team member jeopardizing everyone by throwing a fit and walking off the mountain when things aren't going smoothly.

Now ask yourself—why would a director want and need anything less on an "artistic expedition?" Are you the type of person a director would choose to bring on the climb of her "artistic Everest?" Are you that kind of actor/team member? What could you do to become the kind of actor that directors want on their teams?

Keep the drama on stage. — Steven Hauck, actor

Since you have control over your own behavior in the workplace, be the actor everyone wants to work with. You will increase your odds of going on more artistic expeditions. People will want you around. Directors will rely on you because you will have a reputation of being a dependable team player who always brings your "A-Game" to every professional situation. Being a great team member is something you can continually work to improve over the course of your career.

Be a Member of a Team

Exercise: **Give yourself five minutes to do this exercise.**

Recall an event when you were a member of a team. Examples—a church choir, a sports team, a community theatre production, even—dare we say it—a class group project. Choose an endeavor that you consider successful or positive.

What did you appreciate about that experience at the time?

Is there anything new you can appreciate about that experience now?

What qualities did you bring to the process that you felt were valuable?

How could you have been a better member of the team? What, if anything, kept you from being a good team member?

Further Reflection . . .

- **Compare your lists with others who have also done this exercise. What are the common characteristics or traits of a team player?**
- **What made your experiences fulfilling?**

Dispatches from the Field—Lori

When I was an understudy, I worked diligently to make sure my experience was positive. I wanted to do my best when I went on for the lead. There were a lot of people working hard to ensure that the show ran smoothly. I felt that my best efforts would be the only appropriate demonstration of my appreciation and respect for the talent and efforts of all of those involved in the production. The audience also deserved nothing less than my best efforts.

On the first night that I went on for the lead, here's what I did: about ten minutes before the performance, I gave myself a moment alone. I reminded myself of the gratitude I felt for the opportunity to perform. Then I reminded myself of all of the people who were hard at work making that performance happen. Next, I thought about the audience. Without them, we would have been working in a vacuum. It's amazing how many ways you can be grateful when you take a moment to consider all the factors and people involved in bringing a performance to life. Gratitude and awareness make me a better team player.

If you view yourself as part of a team, your success is shared with others and you will feel more connected to your colleagues. You can describe this process in all kinds of ways: appreciating, connecting, empowering, honoring, celebrating, and much more. Whatever name you give it, it's important that you recognize that it's about the interconnected nature of your work as an artist/actor. You have the opportunity to feel connected as a team, and it may lead you to experience your work as more rewarding. Singers in a choir and athletes on a team rely on the collaborative spirit of the group. The end-product requires the skills, energy, and commitment of many. The results are greatest when everyone does their best work and contributes positively. You have the opportunity to influence a small or large group in a variety of ways through the collective efforts of you and your colleagues. We invite you to take a moment and consider this before your next performance.

If you are more appreciative of the people, the opportunity, and the process involved, it might be easier to see your work as being of service. The process demands that you take the focus off yourself and recognize that your success depends on other people and that the project is greater than any individual.

Here are some things to think about:

- Respect the other players on the team—everybody is needed to make a team. You are only one member of the team; without others you wouldn't be so special.
- If you are the leader, you are not the only one on the team. Those around you are leaders as well. Take the time to assess the

specific skills of each member and allow everyone to bring their expertise to the process.

- Encourage those around you to be good leaders as well.

Great Qualities in Teammates

Exercise: **Think of five people with whom you've enjoyed working. It could be a fellow actor from a show or class project, a friend at a part-time job, or a fellow volunteer. It could also be a boss, director, coach, or leader.**

Write the names of the five people in the far-left column of the chart below.

One at a time, take each name on your list and ask yourself what made that person enjoyable to work with.

Write out five exceptional characteristics or traits that each person you listed brought to the job. You will have twenty-five traits listed in total (some may be repeated).

We have created an example in the chart with John Jones to get you started.

Enjoyable Person at Work	Exceptional Trait	Exceptional Trait	Exceptional Trait	Exceptional Trait	Exceptional Trait
John Jones	Patient	Thoughtful	Funny	Articulate	Good listener

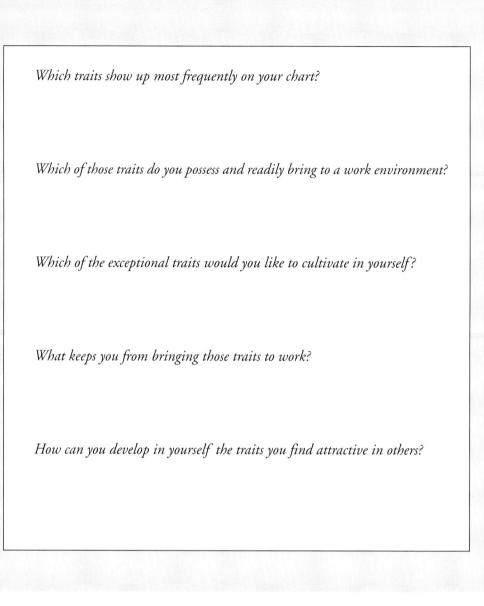

Which traits show up most frequently on your chart?

Which of those traits do you possess and readily bring to a work environment?

Which of the exceptional traits would you like to cultivate in yourself?

What keeps you from bringing those traits to work?

How can you develop in yourself the traits you find attractive in others?

Be an exceptional person when you show up to work and earnestly contribute your best efforts to the goals of your team. One way to positively contribute to your work situation is to show genuine concern for your coworkers' well-being. If someone on your team is being "edgy" and behaving in a way that impacts the group negatively, decide not to stoke the fire. Something as simple as asking that person if everything's okay could help shift her attitude. Perhaps your coworker will wake up and take responsibility for minding her edge and stop inflicting it on others. Decide to have compassion toward your coworkers instead of inflaming situations, snapping back, or pushing people away. You'll be surprised how your attitude impacts others. The concern you genuinely show for others will make you feel better and more connected to the team, and that concern can be contagious.

Making a commitment to minding your edges and being the actor everyone wants to work with will require you to develop an awareness of your behavior as well as that of others. You've probably already run into a lot of unique characters on your path. We'd like to point out a few characteristics of some of the possibly challenging "edges" you may encounter in yourself and those around you.

MINDING THE "EDGY" EDGES

Imagine being stuck with an "edgy" actor for weeks on a frozen, windy mountain. Some actors believe that because they are brilliant, creative, insightful, or funny, they're automatically granted the right to have an attitude and to undermine others. They can be denigrating and sarcastic under the guise of being "funny." It's clear they are hurting others and destroying the positive collective energy. It's not fun to be around them because we don't trust them. The bottom line is that no one deserves to be treated with anything less than respect. Remember, "attitude" usually masks insecurity.

MINDING THE "NASTY" EDGES

How can work ever be fulfilling when the environment is toxic? Ask yourself if you are contributing to the toxicity in any way. When you are having a bad day, it doesn't mean that someone else should have to pay the price for it. Leave it at the door! If you find yourself in a job where the work environment is negative and difficult, greet it with a pleasant face. Others will have a hard time being nasty to a centered, genuinely pleasant person.

MINDING THE "CHIP ON THE SHOULDER" EDGES

Beware of the actor who always seems to have a gripe about things being "unfair" and how he is not getting what he deserves. This attitude often stems from feeling overlooked and missing out on what he believes belongs to him. This actor is filled with jealousy. This person makes it his mission to be noticed at all costs and will often bully others. If you can, just move out of the way—let him pass you by. Don't stick around to be the next person to receive an earful.

MINDING THE "NEEDY" EDGES

No one likes working with a needy actor, and most needy actors can't admit they are being needy. Just in case you're wondering if you fit into this category, we have a quick test for you to take. Be honest with yourself. This test is done in the privacy of your own mind, so no worries—no one else is going to see it.

The Needy Person At-Home Test Kit

Exercise: **If you answer yes to any or all of
these questions, you *might* be a needy person.**

Do you need *constant praise, attention, or approval?*

Do you need *to be involved in every conversation or be the center of
attention socially?*

*Do you find that you're just waiting for your turn to add to a conversation
rather than genuinely listening to others?*

Do you have a laundry list of accommodations that must be met by others in order for you to work effectively? Do you secretly keep this list to yourself and expect others to meet your expectations without ever telling them?

Are you certain you're not needy, it's just that you know exactly what is required for you to work at your optimal level? Do you make those demands without considering the needs of others?

Dispatches from the Field—Lori

It's a little embarrassing to look back at the times when I have been a needy actor. One particular instance comes to mind and it makes me cringe. I was on the road and we had a one-night performance. The crew arrived earlier in the day, and we were scheduled to perform that night. I kept pestering the stage manager with my list of "needs" for the performance. I didn't take into account the fact that he, too, had just arrived and had many responsibilities to make the show a success, including attending to other actors' needs. In hindsight, I wonder what I could have done to make his job easier instead of fretting about my needs. We were in a new theatre and everyone, including me, had to make adjustments and be flexible.

Needy actors are often tedious people who zap the energy and creativity from the process, monopolize situations, and frustrate others. Needy people generally battle low self-esteem and will attack when they feel threatened or challenged by others. The productive alternative to being needy is being flexible. Flexibility is a must in any situation. Being able to roll with change and uncertainty allows you to mind your own edge.

Chapter 10

The Circle of Work

The Ongoing Process

*F*or the bulk of people in the mainstream world of work, finding employment is a linear endeavor.

seek work → interview → land job

It is a straight line that begins at "seek work" and ends at "land job." Once the job seeker has secured a position the process is complete. The expectation is that he or she won't have to worry about the threat of unemployment in the near future. This is not the case for an actor. As you build your career, you will discover that one aspect of your job is the continual pursuit of work. We propose that actors think of bending the traditionally linear process into a circle. We call it the *Circle of Work*. This is a paradigm that will empower you to develop strong, effective habits in the *continual* process of finding work.

The Circle is a sequence of stages that can be used as a means by which you can assess your efforts and your forward movement. Hopefully, it will inspire you to create new opportunities.

The Circle of Work operates like this: seek work, audition, get a callback, book the job, do the work, celebrate and feel the satisfaction of a job well done, and finally, assess the work and recharge. The cycle then starts all over again with "seek work." As a working actor, the stages of the Circle of Work overlap. That is, even when you are "at work" you must always be seeking work. Use the diagram below as a tool to help you keep your actions forward moving. Remember, there is always a next step.

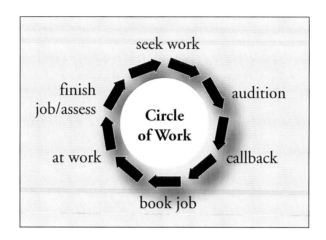

Let's take a closer look at each element in the Circle of Work.

- *Seek Work:* Examples of seeking work include reading the trade papers and online casting notices from services like *Backstage* and *Actors' Access.* This also means researching upcoming projects on such sites as Broadwayworld.com and Variety.com to find out about projects that might be right for you. Being knowledgeable about what's happening in "the business" is critical when talking with industry professionals. If you are informed about the industry then you will present yourself as a serious professional. Networking is a great way to enhance your opportunities to find work, and every situation is a networking opportunity. (We'll talk more about networking in chapter 12.) In a social situation, you may discover an unanticipated connection. In a professional environment, you may hear of potential opportunities as you talk with other actors.

- *Audition:* A traditional way of looking at this aspect of the Circle of Work would be to say that you go to an audition to seek employment. This is basically a job interview to see if you fit the needs of a specific project. As an actor this is also an opportunity to build relationships. A good audition increases the odds that you will come to mind for future projects. Even if you don't book the job, you have put yourself in line for future possibilities. You would be surprised how often a job opportunity will come to you from "out of the blue" because you met someone while auditioning for another project. Continue to show up, do great auditions, and build relationships.

- *Callback:* Ah, the callback. An opportunity to return and see the people who liked you in the first place. Remember this important fact—*they liked you.* If they didn't, why would they waste everyone's valuable time by bringing you back? Unless you have been told specifically that you need to change something (your hair, clothes, character, etc.), allow yourself to feel confident in knowing that they liked what they saw and you don't have to reinvent yourself. What you brought to the original audition got you a callback. Callbacks are important triumphs. You are creating a reputation, and that callback is evidence that you've got what it takes. If you are being disciplined in your thinking you will understand that this is forward motion—momentum. A callback should be a confidence builder. Yes, it would be nice to get the job, but don't allow the victory of a callback to go unacknowledged.

- *Book the Job:* You did it! Enjoy this step and celebrate. Share your success with those who support you and have your best interest at heart. They will want to celebrate with you. Share your enthusiasm in a way that inspires others. Hard work and disciplined habits pay off. Let your success be an example of what others can achieve. Allow your success to motivate others, and allow yourself to be motivated by their successes as well.

- *At Work:* This is where you roll up your sleeves and do exactly what you have been trained to do: exercise your artistic muscles and realize your passion. You have the opportunity to demonstrate your artistic disciplined habits as well as your ability to be the person everyone wants on their team. You've fulfilled your desire to be a working actor and you are practicing your craft.

Be sure to invite industry people to see your work. Your performance can be an audition that allows you to be seen in a setting where you are at your best—rehearsed, polished, and fully engaged in the storytelling process. Perhaps they will think of you for an upcoming project or recommend you to a colleague. Don't forget that your fellow actors may introduce you to their industry contacts and recommend you for projects, so always do your best to respect those on your team.

- *Finish Job/Assess:* Allow the closing of a show, film, commercial, or other production its due. Acknowledge the work you have done and thank all the people involved. And yes, congratulate yourself if it's a job well done. You did it!

Take a moment to assess the job. Here are some questions to ask yourself:

> *How did this job contribute to my career?*
>
> *What did I gain from this experience? Personally? Artistically? Professionally?*
>
> *Is there anything I would do differently next time?*
>
> *What contacts and professional relationships did I create?*

While you may not think you have the luxury to do so, try to give yourself a breather! Assess how much down time you need before you start working again. If a project was especially difficult or emotionally taxing, determine how you can recharge your battery so that you are at your best and ready to audition again. You may need some time off. Walk in the park, watch a movie, or visit an art museum to get those creative juices flowing again. Only you can assess what you really need to recharge. It could just be a good night's rest.

The Circle of Work allows you to easily assess where you are and to determine how much time you need to devote to each phase. If you look at this chart as a pie, the amount of time you spend in each section of the circle is not equally divided, nor should it be. It will change given the circumstances of your career. You may have a job for two months or be on tour for a year or more. However, a long-term job is not an excuse to take a break from the Circle of Work. The more you seek opportunity, the more likely you will be to find work when that job concludes.

Forward thinking is important no matter what kind of work you get. Let's create a "dream come true" scenario as an example. Say that you are cast in a production—we'll say it's a film. This is a perfect role for you; in fact, you consider it the "role of a lifetime." The film takes four months to shoot, and you are tremendously fulfilled and successful. Eventually the project is complete. Let's say you win lots of awards for your work, and the film catapults you to great visibility with offers for more exciting projects. What happens next? You still have to look for a new acting job. Yes, you may have agents and managers to help you look for work, and your time may be spent reading scripts and choosing the roles you'll play, but you are still involved in the Circle of Work, searching for the next opportunity.

Many actors discover that they are most successful at finding work when they feel confident and aren't desperate for the job. Feeling confident about what you have to offer anchors you and prevents you from defining your self-worth by whether or not you are hired. It's much easier to feel good about yourself and your abilities when you are actively developing and exercising your skills through performance, classes, workshops, and other similar activities. The more confident you are, the more marketable you will be.

Take full advantage of the times when you are riding high and feeling great about yourself. Use the confidence and artistic affirmation you get from being an employed actor to energize your drive and motivation. This is a time to charge ahead rather than pretend that the job will continue forever. Denying the fear of not having a job doesn't make the reality go away. A working actor is perfectly positioned to get out there and seek additional opportunities to work!

When you audition, you are creating relationships, not just seeking a job. Projects can take time to launch and come to fruition. Just because you auditioned for something today doesn't mean the job is going to happen tomorrow or next week. If there isn't a perfect acting position for you from today's audition, trust that if they liked what you brought to the audition, your chances of being considered for future productions will skyrocket.

Seeking Work: A Quick Assessment

Exercise: **Honestly assess your progress when you are in this stage of the Circle of Work.**

How am I actively seeking work?

If I am in an acting job right now, how am I actively looking for my next possible gig as well?

Am I utilizing and maximizing the tools I have at my disposal?
- *Are my resume, headshot, website updated?*
- *Do I use social media to connect with industry contacts?*
- *Do I have postcards to send to industry contacts?*
- *Am I up to date on the industry?*
- *Am I consistently checking for self-submission opportunities?*

What else could I do to create work for myself?
- *Could I collaborate with friends on a new project?*
- *Do I have an idea for a project, a class, a creative endeavor?*

Am I prepared at auditions?

Am I on time for auditions?

Am I doing my best work at auditions and callbacks?
* *If not, what areas need help? Who could I ask for help?*

How do I follow up after I meet industry people?

Am I taking time to assess jobs when I complete them?

Am I feeding my artistic soul with meaningful and challenging activities?
* *If not, what do I need to do to reactivate and connect with my artistry?*

Further Reflection . . .
* **How does the Circle of Work inform your concept of being a working actor?**
* **In what ways does the Circle of Work benefit you?**

Chapter 11

Getting Work

Know What You're Selling

There's always work; you're either working or working at finding work. There is work you're going to get paid for and work you're not going to get paid for, but there's always work. I just started taking guitar lessons because it could become a marketable skill later. I'm going to a premiere of a film tonight, and the time spent with a casting director is work.

You have to keep that flame going, and you need to be relentless. It has to be the most important thing in your life. Have fun with every audition, and job, and the journey at large because it is all going to go by faster than you think.

The people who are working don't have the "grabbing/I must make it" energy. They are really enjoying themselves and are generous with other actors. The energy isn't one of need—it comes from their strength, a strength usually built upon the fact that they generated their own opportunities that lead to more work.

— Adrian Martinez, actor

*M*ost actors would prefer the Circle of Work be comprised of a single step—"at work." That would be great, but the truth is that an integral part of an actor's reality as a freelance artist is the perpetual pursuit of work. The process can be anxiety provoking for many actors at many stages of their careers. This chapter will help you engage in the Circle of Work and provide insights and tips as you explore strategies to becoming a working actor. Once you acknowledge the ongoing nature of the process, you'll discover innovative ways to seek work and use the MTE tools to navigate your life as a successful, fulfilled actor.

In the same way that you have developed a personal system for memorizing lines and a technique for analyzing and understanding a role, implementing Circle of Work strategies can be an important part of your actor toolbox. Adopting this system for being the CEO of your business can empower you to look down the road and see a path rather than the edge of a cliff. And as with every other MTE strategy and tool, you will be using your personal fulfillment needs (PFNs) as the underlying force that drives your actions.

The best time to start implementing the MTE strategies is now. For many of you, now may mean a time when you're in school and safely in the "cocoon" it provides. Being in school gives you the opportunity to develop your business skills without the pressure and responsibility of earning a living. Some student actors may say, "I'm in school—I don't have to worry about getting work now—that comes after graduation!" Nothing could be further from the truth. Now is the time to develop and strengthen your skills before the stakes get higher. Incorporate these principles from the start and you stand a better chance of success. In fact, starting *now* embraces the underlying premise of the Circle of Work—the best time to look for a job is when you already have one. You can experience freedom from neediness when you audition, since you already have a full-time job—it's called school. Since you are already "employed," you won't feel desperate at auditions.

First things first—identify the jobs that are right for you. This is the type of work that is in alignment with your personal fulfillment needs as well as your type. These are the jobs that will take you the furthest in your career and they are the jobs that will be the stepping-stones to career advancement.

> My most important piece of advice for young actors, regarding television auditions in particular, is to bring *yourself* to the character. When you audition for TV, you might be shooting *tomorrow.* You and the character need to be one. Walk in and bring smart acting choices layered on top of *you.* That will be the most believable character you can possibly present, and guess what? The one I believe gets the job.
> — Todd Sherry, actor/casting associate

Have you ever watched a production and thought, "I'm right for that role"? That thought is actually a stepping-stone to identifying the types of roles that are right for you. It's terrific that you see yourself playing specific roles. You don't want to be in fantasyland about the types of roles that are right for you, instead, you want to make sure that the roles you seek make sense for who you are. By looking at yourself realistically and honestly, you can start to identify and market yourself. It's critical that you understand the difference between what you are like inside and how you come across to others as well as the roles that appeal to you versus the roles you can play.

Dispatches from the Field—Carl

Occasionally a student will come to my office after a cast list has been announced. Invariably, the student is disappointed that he was not cast in the role he wanted. Usually, another student actor who was cast was more "right" for the role or fit my particular vision of the part. Several years ago, a student approached me about not being cast in the role of Fastrada in the musical Pippin. *She was clearly upset and broke down in tears in my office. She couldn't understand why she had been passed over for the role. She had yearned to do the part. She said she felt like that role was in her. Physically she was wrong for the role, and the energy that she projected was completely different than you'd expect from the evil temptress who schemes to place her son on the throne of France. She kept insisting that she could play the role, even though she didn't demonstrate what I viewed as appropriate choices in her audition for the production I was directing.*

This was a perfect example of when to recognize and acknowledge jealousy and disappointment. It isn't up to you to determine the director's concept or casting decisions. You will have to come to accept the fact that disappointment goes with the territory. Recognizing it won't diminish the impact, but it will allow you to continue in your career without developing a long list of people you resent because they didn't cast you. You will also find that the more you audition, the more you will see the possibilities for employment. Yes, there will be moments that sting more than others, but your awareness of what you do and how you act on those feelings is the critical part.

If you don't have a clear sense of how you come across and what roles are right for you, then you are setting yourself up for loads of frustration and disappointment. There's a difference between the roles you want and the roles you are right for in a "universal or traditional" sense. Understanding your type is critical to the way you approach the Circle of Work. If you're going after jobs that are right for you, then you're that much ahead of the game. Not knowing your type puts you at a disadvantage. Let us also note that directors occasionally cast "against type," but these are exceptions, not the rule.

Dispatches from the Field—Carl

When I was a young actor I was cast in West Side Story *three times. In every instance, I was cast as a Puerto Rican Shark—I'm of Italian ancestry. While I desperately wanted the chance to play a Jet (the "Americans"), it was never going to happen.*

It was a continual source of agitation for me. Accept your type. It'll keep you from banging your head against a wall in frustration.

Dispatches from the Field—Lori

I used to think that I had to get every job I went out for. In a way, that can be motivating, but what happens when an actor keeps going out for jobs and doesn't get cast? It's deeply disappointing. It can also be very self-destructive if defining yourself as a "winner" or a "loser" depends on whether or not you're hired. This way of thinking is a perfect set-up for low self-esteem. This is definitely a time when disciplined positive thinking needs to be applied—vigorously. I worried that if I didn't book more jobs, my agents would lose faith in me and stop sending me out. Of course, that type of thinking just put more pressure on me at auditions. It was a no-win situation and an ineffective way to conduct my business as an actor.

Eventually, I realized that there were jobs that were right for me. My mind-set changed to me thinking, "Somebody, somewhere must need an actor exactly like me to fit roles that match the skills, talent, looks, and personality I bring to the table." Those are the jobs I began to pursue and the ones I continue to pursue today.

It can be tricky (and perhaps a bit unnerving) to identify your "type." As we've said, it's critical to know it because you then know what roles to pursue. If you understand your type, then you can honestly assess yourself and see yourself without judgment.

Identifying Your Type

Exercise: **Here's a way to set the process in motion.**
Ask yourself the following questions:

Which actors that I've seen on film and television seem like me, have similar energy to mine, or have the same "look" as me?

Which actors or characters on TV and in movies have I been told I'm like?

What kinds of roles do those actors play (for example, smoldering, brooding bad boys/girls, or clean-cut honor students)?

Ask your friends the following question:
If you were going to cast the movie of my life, who would play me?

Go back to chapter 2 and read the personal inventory. Without being aware of it, you may have described your type in the answers you provided. You described your looks, the way you think others see you, the kinds of roles you play, and so forth. The information is there. As you read your inventory, see if your answers paint a picture of you that you may not have considered.

We assume you started or will start your career in a city that suits your current professional needs and provides you with appropriate professional challenges and opportunities.

So, how do you get seen for the roles that are right for you? In a word: research. Find out what opportunities are available to you in your school, your community, and the industry. Empower yourself with information about upcoming jobs. Then, connect what you're selling (your talents and abilities) with the people who are buying (directors and producers). The people who cast and develop projects need to know about you and how to find you. That means that either they know about you from your previous work, someone recommends you to them, or you actively create opportunities to audition for them.

The research step is important. Research the people that you want to work with, the places you want to work, and the projects that might interest you, by using the vast array of research tools available on the Internet, in entertainment publications (we've listed some in the appendix), and by word of mouth. Find out what's happening in the industry, whether that means your current area or in the major entertainment centers of New York, Chicago, and Los Angeles. Research the theatre, film, and television opportunities available for actors. You also want to be aware of industrial jobs, which are generally categorized as training films or corporate performances used for internal company promotions. This could take some time, but you have to do this legwork if you are going to understand the job market.

Once you have done the research, you'll need to know how to use the information to get you closer to landing a job. This is where networking becomes important. Building relationships with other people in the industry happens when you take a class, volunteer at a theatre, or make contacts at social events. We'll discuss networking in the next chapter.

Some of you may read this and think, "All of this would be great if I was living in a major market that had a thriving theatre scene, but I live in a small city where there isn't much going on." The operative word in that sentence is *much*. If there's not *much* then there must be *something*. It may take more work to find it, but the opportunities are there. Do the research and find the small dinner theatres, community theatres, and storefront theatres. Where are they located; to whom do you need to talk; what's the best way to contact them? Then take the bull by the horns and make the connection. Reach out and let them know you're available and interested. Make sure you know something about the theatre—upcoming shows, their season, directors—so that when you speak to someone involved with that company, your knowledge will communicate your serious interest in their work. You want to be informed, and that type of information is very easily accessible on the Internet. This is also a way to get in the practice of identifying and pursuing the work you want. Although this is all on a smaller scale than New York or LA, the process is similar, and it will help you bolster your courage and add to your experience if you move on to a larger market.

If you are just starting out as an actor, you should view your age as an advantage and seek opportunities that play into that advantage. There are many roles that require young actors. Producers may be looking for a fresh face that hasn't yet been identified with a product or an established role on TV or film. You can be the "it" they seek. Theatre for young audiences frequently hires twenty-something actors to play teenagers and even children. Research and consider children's theatre companies. Send your resume to them. There is work for young actors, but you have to put yourself out there if you're going to get it.

Make sure that the materials you send to agents, directors, theatres, and casting directors is top notch. Your headshot needs to be done by someone recommended by industry experts in that city. A headshot that works in Chicago may not be the "look" they want in LA. But no matter the city, your resume needs to look polished, your cover letters need to be printed on quality paper, and your business cards have to look professional. The catch-22 in this is that all of this takes money and can be fairly expensive. But remember, if you are not representing yourself as someone who is at the top of his or her game, it's highly unlikely that you'll be considered for a role.

> Be pleasantly persistent and persistently pleasant.
> — Karl Kippola, actor

Utilize any connections you may have when you submit a resume. Send it to someone you know or have met, asking him to pass your resume along to the appropriate person. If you are referred by a casting director or someone in "the business," write "referred by [the person's name]" on the front of the envelope in large letters.

In the appendix we've listed the titles of books that have useful advice about resumes, cover letters, and identifying your type.

STUDENT FILMS

We would like to put in a plug for working with young filmmakers. There are a number of great reasons to act in a student film including practicing your craft, getting footage of your work, and developing relationships. Today's student directors and producers are the next generation of filmmakers and industry leaders. Team up with them now and collaborate. You may become their favorite actor, and down the road, when they are making their feature films or innovative TV series, you will be the actor they call for the role that is perfect for you.

Doing student films (even if you're not a student) is a great way to get film for your demo reel. Compile the best of your student film scenes and edit a short reel (think of it as an advertisement for yourself). Remember that a reel is comprised only of the work you've done specifically for the camera. You don't want to have recordings of a live production or video of yourself performing a monologue in your apartment. Even if you only want to do live theatre, having a reel means that when you walk into an agent's office, the agent will be able to see highlights of your work. Yes, you can always do a monologue for agents or managers in their office, but that's not the same as giving them the opportunity to see a polished performance. When you make a demo of your work, you have the advantage of putting your best foot forward.

MAKING YOUR OWN WORK

> When you are not hired by someone else, create projects on your own. Let people know what you are working on—it's not bragging; it's keeping people informed of your work.
> — Michael Baron, artistic director/director

> If you find yourself in a dry spell and you're ready to jump off the roof because nobody seems to want to hire you, then stop waiting for the phone to ring and just create your own showcase. I had some enormously long periods in Chicago (sometimes years) where I couldn't even get a callback, so for my own sanity and self-care, I wrote my own shows. The worst thing you can do is let the rest of the world convince you that you're not worthy of being seen, especially if your soul tells you otherwise. You don't need a million dollars or a beautiful state-of-the-art theater. My first one-man show was in the dingy basement of a restaurant, with two light bulbs in the ceiling and old sofas for seating. I paid ten bucks to rent the space, and I had the freedom to create whatever I wanted. It doesn't matter if you can sing or dance. Do an evening of monologues or read aloud from your journal or do an extended improv with your best friend—anything! Don't wait for someone else to showcase your specialness. Take the reins yourself and show the world what you've got. It will keep your artist-self exercised, and maybe even lead to a job. You never know who might hear about your show and buy a ticket.
> — Stephen Wallem, actor

Dispatches from the Field—Lori

Early in my career, I realized the importance of making my own work. I found it gratifying during "dry spells" or when I was performing in a long-running show. I was able to craft my own stories, express my unique perspective, challenge myself to take risks, and collaborate with people I cared about and trusted. It was another outlet for the expression of my artistic passion.

When I lived in Chicago, I developed a close circle of friends and colleagues. I felt their support and always looked for opportunities for us to join forces and put our creative heads together. This is how Carl and I began a long career of collaboration and friendship. I met him when I was in a show he choreographed. I was impressed by his understanding of actors and the creative process. He hired me again for a show he directed and thus began the wonderful story of a long collaborative history. We constantly looked for opportunities to fuel our combined creative energies. I asked Carl to direct my cabaret act. We dreamed up several shows together and finally developed a funny, outrageous, and somewhat offbeat evening of songs we titled Bring No Pet Monkeys. (I told you it was somewhat offbeat.) The lesson here is that when you meet someone on your professional path who ignites a creative spark and a personal connection, keep that friendship. That relationship may hold the possibility for rich and fulfilling creative experiences. In the case of Carl and me, our friendship and working relationship has lasted many years and taken many forms, including the writing of this book.

I had many more rewarding collaborative relationships as my career evolved. I went on to write a one-woman show called Tiger Meat on Tuesdays. When I decided I wanted to explore film and television, I came up with my own short films and financed them with the money I made from my theatre and commercial work. Eventually, I concocted a faux news reporter, Margo Rose Ferderer, who combs New York looking for the next big story and interviewing unsuspecting bystanders about the latest Broadway show or entertainment gossip. I've posted her clips on YouTube and I have tremendous joy in exercising my comedic muscles.

As you can tell, I'm a major advocate of generating your own work. It's a critical component of my professional fulfillment. Given my passion for using a myriad of outlets to explore creativity, it's not surprising that eventually my career path led me to collaborate with Gerard Alessandrini, a man who also founded his career on making his own work. Many projects have humble beginnings, and his was no exception. Here is Gerard Alessandrini's story:

As a young theatre student, Gerard had a passion for musical theatre. He would sit for hours listening to the records of great Broadway performers like Alfred Drake, Gordon MacRae, and Robert Preston—people whose careers he wanted to emulate. He *wrote parody lyrics of the songs these men immortalized and then used those songs to create a small revue that he performed with three friends in New York City. While this revue didn't make him the next Robert Preston, it did lead to a successful 25-year run of the off-Broadway hit* Forbidden Broadway. *For many years, I had the privilege of performing in* Forbidden Broadway *around the world and in the off-Broadway production. The show has garnered many awards including a special Tony Award.*

Recognize the value in creating your own projects, and the potential those projects have in altering your career.

Further Reflection . . .

- **Which ideas or strategies in this chapter did you find useful? Were there any you hadn't considered?**
- **How did the chapter generate ideas that will help you create different strategies for seeking work?**

Chapter 12

Networking

Building Relationships

> You make it happen. It's all you—the energy you put out into the ether, the new relationships you actively make, the "detective work" you do (round the clock), the thorough preparation, and an attitude of gratitude. Together, all of these pieces set you up for the crazy ride that is creating your art. How empowering!
> — Margo Seibert, actor

*Y*ou already have a common interest with most folks in the entertainment industry—you enjoy acting and the arts. Since the engine that drives the Circle of Work is "seeking work," we're going to explore how networking skills create audition opportunities.

NETWORKING—THAT DIRTY LITTLE WORD

Networking is something every actor must do. Unfortunately, networking has all sorts of negative connotations. What does networking really mean? For some actors, networking is a frightening concept and an even more repellant action. Well, no wonder. There are a myriad of negative images and stereotypes in our culture that surround networking.

Let's envision networking at its most horrifying extreme. Visualize yourself as the socially awkward stereotypical salesman forced to sell a superbly crappy, useless product to unreceptive yet potential clients. Envision yourself in this worst-case scenario of networking. Feel how embarrassing it is and notice that those around you are ridiculing you because you act like a jerk, suck up, brown nose (or whatever makes you cringe). Got that image? Okay—let it go.

Now think of an artist who has just designed the most unique piece of jewelry or painted a magnificent painting. It's his "baby." He wants to make sure it winds up in the hands of the right owner. What if there are lots of buyers for this "product" that he just created? That artistic "salesperson" has a personal interest in the piece of jewelry or painting because he designed it and put his heart and soul into its creation. It's no different for an actor. If you have faith in yourself and what you have to "sell," then why would it be terrible or intimidating to want to share it with others?

Now think of someone in your life who is a great "people person"—someone whom others love to be around. She's like a people magnet. She is comfortable with herself and makes those around her feel at ease. This is someone you want to spend time with at a party or have as a friend. She is fantastic at networking. Does she call it networking? Probably not. Being an engaging, interesting person who reaches out to others comes naturally to her, so most likely she doesn't think about her inherent networking ability.

How are you when you are in a room with people who have the power to hire you? If you are in a social setting, do you become like "Brendon," the mysterious, melancholy "artiste," wearing a beret and hiding in the corner, believing he should never have to stoop so far as to engage with others in order to sell himself? Or, are you like "Brenda," the freckle-faced redhead in a low-cut top licking her lips, laughing inappropriately and ready to go home with whoever asks her? Of course, these are extremes, but both of these behaviors will probably not be the way you would like to conduct the business of landing jobs.

It might be helpful to ask yourself how you would like others to act around you if you were in the position to hire them. You probably wouldn't want to hire someone who avoided you in a social setting or work with someone who was constantly in your face trying to manipulate you.

Industry professionals like to hire and be around actors who are interesting, engaging people, not those who strive to be something they think others want them to be. The goal is to be at ease when you're in professional situations. How does an actor become effective at networking? First, you need to be comfortable being you. This will put those around you at ease as well. As you go through your daily life, you're not playing a character; you are being yourself—your authentic, real self. You are naturally attractive when you are comfortable in your own skin and allow the real *you* to shine through.

It might seem difficult at first. You may feel uncomfortable. You may feel as though you're trying to "sell yourself," and therefore your interactions may feel forced. This can be especially challenging when you are interacting with people who are in the position to hire you. Think of networking as putting your best foot forward in a social situation. How would you interact if a potential job weren't factored into the equation? If the person you're meeting weren't "connected" in the industry or in a position to hire you, what would you say?

Here are some suggestions that may help you when you are in a networking situation.

- Ask questions. "What are you working on right now? That sounds interesting. Tell me about it."
- Walk into a situation with three "generic" personal or professional topics you can discuss with someone.
- Here is an opportunity to use the "elevator speech" we'll discuss later in the chapter.
- Learn to talk about topics other than you—art, current events, science, travel, restaurants—get into a genuine conversation.

What makes you interesting? "My life isn't that interesting," you say. But it is. You come from a family with a story—everyone's family has its own story and history. You live in a specific location with specific types of people around you. You have unique perspectives and opinions about the world around you and those belong exclusively to you. Networking doesn't have to be difficult. It's about making conversation. Don't you feel good when someone listens to you and shows a genuine interest in getting to know you? Simple discussions about your favorite take-out sushi place or stories about "what the funny guy in front of me at the grocery store did last week" are ways we casually connect with others. It isn't rocket science and you don't even have to talk about "heady topics" to express who you are to others. You don't have to be fascinatingly knowledgeable about the industry. You don't have to be filled with compliments for the person with whom you are speaking. Engage, listen, share, pay attention to nonverbal cues, and be positive in a sincere and genuine way.

If you think of networking as seed planting rather than soliciting, you may have an easier time with it. Networking is relationship building. There's the famous quote about success in "the business"—"it's all about who you know." This does not have to mean you begin your life as an actor knowing Broadway producers, film directors, and top-tier agents. It means that you recognize the power of creating relationships. In the beginning, you may not know where they will lead, but you can be sure that the more professional relationships you create, the wider the net you cast, and that will translate to more opportunities to be hired.

Networking doesn't necessarily mean you walk around handing out your resume. It does mean you always have your business card on hand—and you ask others for theirs. It means you express genuine interest in the work and the life of others. It means you listen and extend yourself in polite conversation at social gatherings and parties. Networking means you celebrate the success of others and avoid competition or jealousy when you engage with those who are further along in their careers.

Networking is also about what kind of job you take to support yourself; I always say it's better to be a waiter in a restaurant where theatre people or TV and film people go than to be in an office where you're the only one in the arts. I can't tell you how many waiters and waitresses I called in to audition. It may seem difficult or embarrassing to work at a place that's filled with people from "the business," but you're more likely to meet someone there who can help you out. It doesn't mean you push yourself on anyone, but if you're charming and fun and really good at your job, you may get noticed. Also, you'll probably be working around other actors and that's a very important part of networking. And then there's taking classes: I tell actors that if they're going to take a class, go to one where a sizeable number of the actors actually work, a class where the actors have agents—don't go to some class where the students have been there for ten years and every once in a while someone gets an under-five on a soap opera and only two people have agents. As you make friends in the class, someone will, at some point, say, "you should meet my agent."
— Gary Dontzig, writer/producer

Dispatches from the Field—Lori

A complaint I have heard from actors just starting out is that they don't know anyone in "the business." It can feel very discouraging. I'm here to tell you that I didn't know anyone in "the business" when I started. There were no Equity theatres, TV shows, feature films, or commercials being shot when I was growing up in New Salem, North Dakota (population 1,000). But, as I said before, that didn't stop my mom from finding performance opportunities (when I was too young to do it on my own) and later for me to find my own opportunities. That is how I set my foot on each and every stepping-stone that has led me to where I am today. So what I'm saying is that if I can do it starting from where I was, so can you. It is a process. Start now, hang in there, and keep building up your circle of friends and fans in the industry.

THE ELEVATOR SPEECH

An *elevator speech* can be helpful when someone asks you the question, "What's going on?" or "What are you working on?" Your elevator speech is a personal "update" that can be told to someone in the length of time it takes to ride an elevator to the seventh floor. It is not a laundry list but an expression of what engages you at the moment. It reflects your passion and interest. It speaks not only about the way you occupy your time but also the energy those endeavors provide you. When used in a business setting, your elevator speech could help others see how you might fit into their projects. Here's an example of one of Lori's elevator speeches about a project she discussed earlier in the book.

> I worked on the "Onion News" and decided I wanted to do some Comedy Central-type spokesperson work. So, I created a reporter character named Margo Rose Ferderer, and I'm filming "man on the street" videos. It's a blast. You wouldn't believe some of the footage we got!

Here's an elevator speech one of Carl's students used when she graduated from AU.

> I'm graduating from AU in May and plan to stay in DC for a year. For our senior capstone, my class wrote and produced an original musical version of *Lysistrata*. We're rewriting and entering it in Fringe Festivals. I never fully grasped a musical's power to move an audience.

Notice that each elevator speech is personal and specific. While there's some "generic" information in the AU alum speech—graduating in May, staying in DC—there is also some specific, engaging information that highlights the actor's passion, his willingness to discover and learn new things, as well as his motivation and initiative.

If you don't have an elevator speech, now is the time to develop one.

Create Your Elevator Speech

Exercise: **There are lots of ways to invent an elevator speech. If you're having trouble getting started, try this format and create one of your own. We'll use the example of Carl's former student from AU.**

Step 1: Write a fact that's a recent (*I just graduated from AU . . .*) career-focused accomplishment.

Step 2: Add a statement that reflects a specific insight into what you are doing. (*Working on a musical version of* Lysistrata *for a senior project.*)

Step 3: Write a statement that expresses a passion, interest, or perspective about your work in alignment with your PFNs. (*I never fully grasped a musical's power to move an audience.*)

As you continue to have new ideas, projects, and passions, your elevator speech will change to reflect what's happening in your life. You will need to continually update and modify your elevator speech. You may find that you need two elevator speeches: one for people who know you and one you use when you meet someone for the first time.

Be creative and have fun with it. It's a wonderful networking tool!

Dispatches from the Field—Carl

One of the most dreaded questions a senior in college has to hear is, "What are you doing after graduation?" Often, acting students will answer with a brief, mumbled reply such as, "I'm going to New York to be an actor. I'll probably wait tables and look for work." The subject is awkwardly dropped and both parties politely move on to another topic. Either that or the listener then describes his or her perceived horrors of life as an actor. A prepared elevator speech is an empowering tool when someone asks the "dreaded question." Your answer demonstrates that you are focused on your career goals. And while you may not state it explicitly, your statement shows that you are in pursuit of your personal fulfillment needs.

Further Reflection . . .

- **How often do you use your elevator speech?**
- **In what ways have you altered the speech?**

Chapter 13

Freaking Out

Managing Your Anxiety

> During the downtimes in your career, take the time to learn
> how to do something that is calling you or for which you
> have a passion and can find a way to use it in your craft. In
> order to have the emotional access you need, you must live a
> full life. Your life experience will inform your artistry since
> there is no cookie-cutter way to do it. Take the focus off
> "let me get famous" and focus on the artist you want to
> become and the art you want to create.
> — Saidah Ekulon, actor

Dispatches from the Field—Carl

As a means of helping young actors transition to the world of professional acting, Lori and I piloted this book by including it as one of four textbooks in a course I taught at American University about the business of show business. The class focused on the kind of skills and perspectives that we described in the first few pages of the book. In addition to the other textbooks, we had numerous visits from professionals: actors, directors, a small nontheatrical business owner, and an advertising agency vice president were guest speakers. We wanted the students to think of their careers as businesses and hear important viewpoints and advice from a variety of professionals. After a few weeks of teaching the class, I began to recognize a pattern of behavior from the students. They would intermittently seem disengaged or zoned out—not every student during every class—but eventually all of them got "the look." They took turns getting a sort of glazed look in their eye. I was surprised. These were students I'd taught before. Most of them had done exemplary work in my classes. Then I began to question my teaching. Was I not providing useful information? Was it repetitive? Were they unable to see the real-world application of the concepts? So, I asked them point blank to tell me what was going on. Their response floored me. They were freaked out by the fact that they hadn't considered these concepts, responsibilities, and tasks. They had never thought about themselves in the particular light I presented—they were "actors." How were they ever going to learn to do all of these things? There was too much to think about. Why hadn't anyone ever told them this before?

So, I moved on with that information planted firmly in my mind. On occasion, there were meltdowns during my office hours and outbursts in class when students vented their frustrations about the tough road ahead, but at the end of the semester they all knew what to expect from the "cold, cruel world." So much of fear is about not knowing. Their freak-outs came from being overwhelmed by how much they needed to do to prepare themselves to meet the challenges of the industry. I reminded them that no one said they had to accomplish everything in one day or even one semester. When they began to embrace the concepts in this book (as well as the other texts), I could see that they were visibly less overwhelmed. Everyone is allowed to freak out. The point of this book is that you'll be armed with some useful information and strategies so you harness and cope with your panic or anxiety rather than just spin out of control.

Sometimes issues of anxiety are challenging enough that you may need to seek professional help. If you find that the stress of your career is taking a toll, make sure you have a conversation with a physician, a therapist, or another health care professional who can recommend a course of treatment. There are also simple stress reducers like yoga, meditation, and exercise. Something as simple as deep breathing is a good place to start when you're wound too tightly.

It may be helpful for you to identify and label the emotions and feelings that make you feel stuck or overwhelmed. If you can name the emotion you're experiencing, it can help you be in charge of it and not let it rule you. The following examples are intended to help you name the cause of your freak-out. If you name the feeling and the source, you can put it in perspective and that may make it easier to handle what's currently on your plate.

Freaking out happens for all kinds of reasons. In our experience, we've noticed that there are a variety of ways people freak out. Here are three that we've consistently encountered: "energy-draining," "energy-dead," and "energy-consuming" freak-outs. "Energy-draining" freak-outs (feeling sad, defeated) cause you to withdraw, give up, mope, and say "forget it." "Energy-dead" freak-outs (feeling like a deer in the headlights) produce a mind-numbing state that leaves you shutdown and paralyzed with indecision. "Energy-consuming" freak-outs (feeling overwhelmed, inundated, panicky) happen when you "spin in circles" with lots of questions, anger, and frustration—it all comes at you so fast that you get worked up into a state of panic and anxiety. Have you experienced any (or all) of them? In all of these situations, you are unable to think rationally or focus logically on the issue at hand. Any of these situations has the potential to derail and undermine you on your path to success and fulfillment.

Dealing with the "Freak-Outs"

Exercise: **The next time you are in freak-out mode, try the following steps—these and a few long, deep breaths may help you feel more centered.**

- *Identify the feeling. What do you feel? Be specific.*
  "I feel sad, stuck, overwhelmed . . ."

- *Why are you freaking out? What's causing it? Did something specific trigger this?*

  "Everyone knows where they'll move after graduation and I don't."

- *What would alleviate the problem? Is there something that could happen to make the freak-out disappear or diminish? Think outside of the box—even if it sounds outlandish.*

  "I need to know where I'm going to live."

- *What steps can you take (even baby steps) to move toward diminishing the problem?*

  "I can begin to research my options."

Dispatches from the Field—Carl

When a student is having a meltdown, we go through the above steps together. The example answers above are based on the following true discussion. One young woman came to my office freaking out. "I don't know where to go after graduation!!!!! How am I supposed to know if it's better to move to New York or stay in DC?" I asked her how she felt, and she said, "freaked out." I asked her to tell me what that meant. After a few minutes, we acknowledged that she felt overwhelmed by the decision. There was too much information and she had no idea how to sort it out. She didn't know if she was moving toward a good decision. What if she made the "wrong" decision? She had been in conversation with a few peers who had postgraduation plans.

She didn't have one yet. I asked her what would alleviate the problem. I was amused when she said she wanted someone else to make the decision (she really didn't want this, but she wanted some guidance). In her mind, handing the decision over to someone else meant an objective decision would be reached. "I told her she needed to thoughtfully examine the pros and cons of living in both cities. She asked me how she was supposed to do that. It was a huge job. Yes, it was a huge job, but spiraling out of control wasn't the alternative to taking the time, step by step, to consider the options, do the research, and connect with her personal fulfillment needs and her goals. The answer wouldn't show up instantly, but with every new fact and piece of the puzzle, she was moving closer to an answer.

WHEN FREAKING OUT MEANS "I'LL NEVER WORK AGAIN"

There will be times when you feel stuck in the "Seek Work" portion of the Circle of Work. What do you do if you aren't getting auditions or callbacks? These are probably the toughest times to stay positive and motivated. You don't want to turn your auditions into a "do or die" situation. There is a saying that casting people "can smell desperation." You want those with the power to hire you to see you at your best—relaxed, creative, and present.

It can be a real challenge to keep your confidence level high when you experience a lot of rejection and feel like you are spinning your wheels. This is a time when you need to be proactive and take care of your artistic soul!

> **One must feed the artistic soul. Learn to bake, paint, cook, sew, knit—some artistic expression one can have control over!**
> **— Karen Murphy, actor**

Get fired up by actively engaging your creativity. Confidence and excitement are contagious and empowering. This is a great time to make your own work. Organize play readings once a week at your apartment. Start or join an improv group—shake it up! This is an excellent time to create work of your own that highlights your talents and puts you in your best light. Write a one-person show; create a film, TV pilot, or monologue showcase. Invite your friends to help you. Using the Internet, you can put your work out in the world to potentially be seen by millions. As you ignite your confidence and imagination, you will bring these attractive qualities to your auditions.

> Journal any and all thoughts, frustrations, or impressions
> in order to maintain and cultivate your own point of view,
> and hopefully, you'll be able to inject that into your
> work as an artist so that you can remain in the present
> moment to the greatest extent possible.
> — Kristine Zbornik, actor

Chapter 14

Office Mates

Building Your Team

*N*o successful business runs smoothly without people committed to the mission of that business. The same should be true for your business. As the CEO of your own company, you will need to identify people who will be your "teammates." A supportive team can help you stay focused on your goals and increase the odds for success. We call these team members *Office Mates*.

No one does it alone, especially actors whose careers have any longevity. You have the opportunity to create your own support team to challenge and motivate you. You may already utilize teammates in your personal life: workout partners, study groups, and study buddies are all examples. We establish these specialized relationships to help us accomplish mutual goals. Adding an Office Mate to the infrastructure of your business will provide you with an added boost that can enhance your success. An Office Mate can provide support, accountability, encouragement, and advice as you to move toward your goals.

How do you identify a potential Office Mate? Choose your Office Mate from a pool of like-minded peers. By doing this, you will organize a highly specialized team comprised of artists who are on a similar path and therefore understand the specific career challenges and complexities that you face. If you already have a supportive structure in place with family and friends, keep nurturing and appreciating those relationships. These are the people who have been there for you and will continue to be by your side as you experience the highs and lows of your career. While your boyfriend, girlfriend, partner, or spouse may seem like a logical choice as an Office Mate, it may be more effective to choose people for that role who can be more objective.

There are certain qualities an Office Mate needs to have and certain qualities that aren't ideal in an Office Mate. We'll help you figure that out in the following exercise. Discernment is the key.

Identifying a Potential Office Mate

Exercise Part I: **Make a list of acting peers you like and who share the same or similar challenges that you face: they need to have the capacity to empathize with you. Put every name on the list that fits this description.**

Now examine each name as you ask yourself these questions:
- *Is this person supportive?*
- *Does this person respect you and your talents?*
- *Does this person believe in your potential as an actor?*
- *Has this person earned your respect?*
- *Do you believe in this person's talents and potential?*
- *Do you think this person is a disciplined, focused actor?*
- *Do you celebrate each other's success?*

As you refine your list, delete the names of anyone who you feel:
- *Competes with you*
- *With whom you may compete (this includes competing for roles)*
- *Might belittle or diminish your dreams/goals*
- *Is overly negative*
- *Needs to prove they are always right*

The point of finding an Office Mate is to build the best possible support team that will empower you to reach your career goals. An Office Mate must be someone in whom you can confide and from whom you can expect support.

Review your list of "Potential Office Mates." As you read each name on your list, ask yourself how you honestly feel when you are with each person. Be willing to look at the overall effect the person has on you. Listen to yourself and trust your gut. While there is nothing wrong with being friends with everyone on your list, it's important to realize that you are looking for the best choice to play the role of encouraging teammate.

Be discerning about whom you allow in your inner circle. Do not include anyone who is destructive or undermining. Overly needy people may demand that you do all the supporting and energizing, leaving you feeling drained and used. Sarcastic or cynical people can be incredibly funny and entertaining, but you may not want them around when you are feeling vulnerable, disappointed, or confused. These are the "wolves in sheep's clothing" and you deserve better than that. You want to be with others who are *minding their edges,* and leave behind those who would just as soon push you off a ledge.

Choose your Office Mate from the remaining names on the list you just created. Even if you have only one name on your list, you're in great shape. The good news is that you know what type of person you are looking for to be an Office Mate. If you don't have anyone on the list, then you will need to broaden your search as you seek like-minded people and build your team. This may take a while, but it is better to have people who are in your corner than those who could potentially sabotage you with negativity and competition. Don't give up on finding the right Office Mate—it's a process. You will eventually attract the right team for you.

Getting Started with Your Office Mate

Exercise Part II: **Contact the first person on your list and explain to him or her that you're creating a support team to provide structure and accountability for your career. If he or she is interested, available, and excited by this prospect, then you each have an Office Mate, and you can get to work.**

First you need to create Office Mate "ground rules." Define a framework based on what both of you need from an Office Mate. Here are some guidelines and ideas:

Begin by meeting in person, on the phone, or via the Internet:
- Discuss goals/dreams/vision.
- Set long- and short-term goals.
  Be clear about your vision of success and fulfillment.
- Determine an action plan to work toward those goals.

Establish a weekly/bi-weekly check-in system (you may do it less frequently over time):
- On the phone
- In person
- Via e-mail

At each check-in:
- Discuss what you've each accomplished/done since last meeting.
- Determine the tasks you'll complete before the next meeting.
- Describe the challenges you face.
- Share the feelings/emotions you discovered in the visualization exercise on pp. 37–39 in chapter 2. Describe how you are identifying and experiencing fulfillment in your current situation.
- Make it a goal to improve your listening skills.

Once you establish an Office Mate relationship and set up an initial meeting, you will both still be responsible for achieving your individual goals. Now that you have an Office Mate, you have an opportunity to share the process with a partner. Use the following exercise to generate tasks and goals you can work on together. You will discover other applicable topics as you and your Office Mate develop a working relationship. Remember to keep it positive, encouraging, and forward thinking at all times. Don't shoot down each other's ideas and goals. Instead, examine and suggest ways to refine and improve them.

Office Mate Topics

Exercise Part III: **Read through the following suggested topics with your Office Mate. Which topics/tasks resonate with you right now? Choose those areas as your starting point. With input from your Office Mate, organize your topics into a viable, personal game plan that will effectively move you toward your goals. Build accountability into your plan with your check-ins.**

Goals and my personal fulfillment needs. (Utilize blank pages in the back of the book as necessary.)

How do your current goals address your PFNs?

What are your specific goals? (It's one thing to state your goal as, "I want acting jobs," versus "I want to perform in musicals.")

What strategies have you identified to achieve your goals? (There's a difference between, "I will look for auditions at local theatres," versus "I will identify theatres that do musicals and target them for auditions.")

Headshots
Who are the current photographers in the city? Have you looked at their portfolios? Have you interviewed any of them?

Resumes
Have you created a resume? Do you have an appropriate resume template? Is your resume prepared in both an electronic and printed format?

Cover letters
What does an actor's cover letter look like? Do you need more than one? Have you created a cover letter?

Finding work
Where are you in the Circle of Work? What are the ways to get work without an agent? Are there opportunities to self-submit? What publications and websites list auditions?

Elevator speech
Have you prepared your elevator speech?
Practice your elevator speech with your Office Mate.

Agents/Casting directors
Who are they? How do they work in your city? Do you need an agent? What's the best plan for getting an agent? Could you intern at an agent's or casting director's office to learn more?

Student films/Creating my reel
How do I get involved in student films in my city? How do I make a reel? How long are acting reels?

Additional topics, tasks, and disciplined habits to include as goals and use when you check in with your Office Mate:
- Read the biographies/autobiographies of actors whose careers you admire.
- Read plays/musicals and listen to sound tracks from shows (the more you know, the more prepared you'll be if you are ever called in for a production).

- Find new material for your audition songbook. Be on the lookout for interesting material that fits who you are and engages you when you sing it.
- Same goes for monologues. Don't be afraid to go outside traditional formats to find them. If you see a film or TV program with a fantastic monologue, transcribe it and add it to your repertoire. (Word of caution—don't use a monologue that is specifically identified with an iconic actor. You want the auditors to see you in the role—not recalling another actor doing the scene. Make sure that if you're auditioning for a play, you use a monologue from a play.)
- Take a class.
- Learn a new skill—especially one you could add to the "special skills" section of your resume.
- Read books written by experts in the field. We've listed several books/resources at the end of this book.
- Get ideas by searching the Internet—looking at the websites, resumes, and reels of actors who are further along in their careers.
- Know your industry. Read trade papers (online or in print) to keep up to date on what's happening in show business in large markets like New York City and LA. Keep track of what's happening in the city you are currently living in. If you're planning a move, be sure to get as much information as possible about that city's acting scene before you arrive.
- Read the newspaper or a news magazine. It's important to be able to talk about something other than the entertainment industry.

Once you determine your goals, report on your success in achieving them. If you tell your Office Mate that you are going to take an acting class and you don't enroll in or audition for one, you will have to admit that you aren't working toward your established goal and you weren't minding the edge. That probably won't feel very good. You also may need to reevaluate your goal: is it doable within the framework you've determined?

OPEN YOUR EARS

Commit to being a better listener. It will serve you well in every aspect of your life, on- and offstage. You've agreed to assist your Office Mate in *minding her edges*, and she will help you mind yours. Listening is a key component in the process. Listening is a skill you have to work at and develop. While it may seem to be an ability that comes naturally to you as an actor, be willing to examine and fine-tune your skill level. Listening isn't about waiting for your turn to speak. Listening requires you to ask questions, probe for clarity, avoid interrupting, and even allow for silence.

Listening requires you to reserve judgment and discover what the other person really means, feels, and thinks. We all have different needs and bring entirely different perspectives, attitudes, biases, and skills to the table. While you will always bring your point of view to any interaction, respect the other person's viewpoint and recognize that everyone sees the world differently.

Listening doesn't necessarily mean that you have to solve a problem. There may be times when you or your Office Mate needs to vent or just needs a sounding board. It's helpful to find out from your Office Mate if she is looking for advice or simply needs to talk. Sometimes an actor needs a safe venue to express her fears, frustrations, and disappointments. Those venues only exist because a relationship is based on trust and support. It's important that your meetings remain positive and don't become gripe sessions. Can you be trusted to listen and empathize? Try to put yourself in the other person's position as empathetically as you can. If you're an actor worth your salt, then you know all about empathy. Also, be sure that your Office Mate is willing to listen as much as she is willing to talk and dispense advice.

If you want a crash course in good listening skills, read what Stephen Covey writes in his book *The 7 Habits of Highly Effective People*: *Habit 5: Seek First to Understand, Then to be Understood: Principles of Mutual Understanding*. It's a concise, comprehensive explanation of the skill. It's wise and well written. You may discover that your improved listening skills will inspire your Office Mate to be a better listener. This is a critical skill to develop. You can even make it a goal.

The Office Mate system is a two-way street. You are going to empower your Office Mate, and in return you need to trust that he or she will "show up" for you. It's important to be genuinely happy for your Office Mate's success. Sometimes this can be tough when you're feeling down or defeated, but by incorporating the MTE philosophy, you can avoid dwelling in a place of jealousy and envy by looking at the bigger picture. When you acknowledge and genuinely celebrate the success of your Office Mate, you invite that kind of success for yourself. There will be an added bonus when it's time to celebrate your success because you will have created a bona fide friend to rejoice with you. If you find that you're not able to celebrate each other's success, or if you are competing with each other in an unhealthy way, you need to find another Office Mate.

You now have a specific structure and some guidelines for the meetings with your Office Mate. Of course, none of this will work unless you are disciplined about it. MTE requires that you enlist your Office Mate to help you consistently and honestly create action plans, assess your progress, and make adjustments along the way. Become a proactive, dynamic pair of allies who provide each other with authentic support.

CREATING AN ACTOR'S PORTFOLIO CHECKLIST

Once you've identified the city where you'll begin your career and have done your research about that city, meet with your Office Mate and discuss the portfolio of tools and documents you will need in your arsenal. In the last chapter we've provided you with a checklist.

Begin by rating yourself on your preparedness. If you think there's room for improvement, then set a goal, create a strategy, and give yourself a timeline for accomplishing the tasks.

Dispatches from the Field—Lori

During my career, I have seen the power of having an Office Mate and how working together is a valuable tool for moving forward. Such is the case with my dear friend, Ruth Bender. We adapted tools she learned at the Actors Information Project. Ruth and I called each other once a week and made a list of ten things we were going to do to advance our careers. This structure helped us support each other to reach our goals and create accountability.

We celebrated the action steps that we took each week rather than focusing only on the result of the actions. If I said I was going to send out three resumes that week and I did, I felt a sense of accomplishment in having done it successfully. I had no control over whether sending out the resumes would lead to auditions or a job, but having done something to move my career forward became a reward within itself. By celebrating the completion of the task, I felt successful, and that feeling gave me the positive energy to take the next action step.

Ruth really supported me when I needed to make sure that industry people came to see me in a show. I had already sent out postcards, and I wanted industry folks to be there. So, Ruth and I devised a plan. She and I sat in my kitchen with the list of the casting directors, agents, and directors I had invited. Ruth dialed them up and said, "This is Ruth Bender calling on behalf of Lori Hammel. I wanted to follow up with the invitation that was sent to you to see Lori in the show. Would you like me to put you on the list for two comps?" Guess what? It worked! The performances were well attended. I felt like I couldn't do it on my own, but with my friend, it became a fun and successful undertaking.

Make the Office Mate model your own. Tailor it to your specific needs and habits. You and your Office Mate may devise your own operating system that's a variation on ours. No matter what form it takes, remember to be realistic, flexible, supportive, and encouraging. Use it as a tool that will make the journey more empowering—a journey you don't have to take alone.

Chapter 15

Make It Work

Setting It All in Motion

*W*e've looked at multiple strategies and a mind-set that will empower you to *mind the edge*, but it's important to see how these concepts integrate into a comprehensive and effective operating system. Hopefully, you have already begun incorporating and applying these ideas and practices to the various steps in Circle of Work. In this chapter, we'll illustrate how to apply our model to your business.

Many actors say that the most challenging step in the Circle of Work is "seeking work." A critical aspect of "seeking work" is relationship building. As we've said, relationship building is the ongoing process of creating and nurturing professional connections. The following illustrates how relationship building can be viewed through a minding the edge perspective.

As we've said, relationship building is the ongoing process of creating professional associations. Let's go through the principles in the book and discuss how you can creatively utilize them when you're building relationships.

MOTIVATION AND RELATIONSHIP BUILDING

Minding the edge means maintaining the drive and sense of purpose that demonstrates you're serious about your work. If you are seriously motivated, you will remain committed when networking seems overwhelming or you don't feel like making the effort to introduce yourself to someone at a party or an industry event. You are MTE when you feel like a slob but decide that a work or social event is too important to dress like one.

FULFILLMENT AND RELATIONSHIP BUILDING

If you're out there building industry relationships, it's probably safe to assume that others, like you, are doing the same thing. See if you can bring your personal fulfillment needs to a networking situation. For instance, if humor is an aspect of fulfillment for you, then bring a humorous perspective to your interactions. You will present a more engaging you. People with similar needs will also gravitate toward you. When you communicate the passion and satisfaction you feel about your projects and opportunities, you are potentially a more appealing person. When the desire to share that passion and satisfaction is a two-way street, you set yourself up for the possibility of creating more genuine relationships that resonate with something deeper than the desire for success, and increase your chances of building relationships based on mutual respect.

DISCIPLINED THINKING
AND RELATIONSHIP BUILDING

The way you approach a situation in your mind is as important as the actions you take in that situation. If you have disciplined thought, you are realistic about your expectations in relationship building. Just because an industry professional agrees to meet with you, it does not mean the person will offer you a job. You are taking steps toward getting a job. You are creating an impression. Generally, people don't meet and get married the next day. Why would you meet someone in a networking situation and assume that he or she will hire you the next day? View your relationship building as "taking steps toward the altar."

Disciplined thought also means you are discerning in your ability to separate advice from discouragement. Let's look at two possible scenarios: (1) Your new agent tells you that you need new headshots as soon as you can afford them (even though you just spent several hundred dollars on the headshots that got you a meeting with this agent in the first place). (2) A fellow actor tells you not to bother contacting a certain casting director because "he never meets with anyone." Which is the advice you want to listen to? Someone who can help you get acting jobs or someone who is jealous and most likely feels discouraged himself? Why forge a relationship with someone who undermines you? Why listen to neg-a-tors who seek to diminish you because they feel competitive or diminished themselves? When you are disciplined in your thinking, you practice discernment in the choices you make regarding the relationships you build and the actions you take.

DISCIPLINED ACTION
AND RELATIONSHIP BUILDING

We've discussed proactive steps that help establish and build professional relationships. Taking these steps requires focus, discipline, and deliberate actions. Below are questions to ask yourself as you seek opportunities to make connections. (You can also use this list as topics for discussion with your Office Mate.) All of the following questions are disciplined actions that will enhance your relationship-building abilities.

- Do I engage with the people in my classes and day-jobs by not only telling them about myself but also expressing an interest in them, their work, and their lives?
- Do I *follow up* when someone says, "Give me a call and we'll talk about . . ." or "Let me know if you have any questions, here's my e-mail address"?
- Have I made lists of the people I know who work in "the business"?
- Am I creating and updating my *Industry Contact List* when I meet people in "the business"?

- Do I ask the people I've met if I could take them to coffee or meet them at their office to genuinely listen to their perspectives and advice?

- Do I follow up with a thank-you note after someone meets with me?

THE 80-YEAR PLAN AND RELATIONSHIP BUILDING

Relationship building requires patience. It is an investment in your future. The payoff isn't always immediate. If you are on the 80-year plan, you understand that seed planting may pay off in ways that are unseen to you in the present. Consider the fact that while you are cultivating positive relationships, those around you are doing the same and they might introduce you to their trusted colleagues and friends.

Recognize that relationships are part of your long-term plan. You appreciate the many possible opportunities your associations will potentially provide in the future. You've heard the phrase, "It's about who you know," but what if it's actually, "It's about someone who knows someone who knows somebody else who introduces you to a person who helps you get your next job"? Even if it isn't clear how an association you make today might be beneficial down the road, consider it to be an investment in the longevity of your career.

BEING OF SERVICE AND RELATIONSHIP BUILDING

On the surface, "being of service" and "relationship building" may not seem to work in tandem, but if being of service is the filter through which you see your career, you will increase the chances of seeking and attracting like-minded people. Being of service requires humility, because the focus is on others as well as yourself. If this becomes your mind-set, then you will reflect this belief not only in the way you behave in work situations but also in the way you choose your words, describe your work, and describe the work of others. When you are building relationships, you are communicating a clear sense of your values regarding work by the way your present yourself. Choose your words with this in mind.

YOU AT WORK AND RELATIONSHIP BUILDING

An ideal situation for relationship building is when you are at work. While you may not know anyone when you start the project, the pressure of talking to strangers or engaging in awkward conversation can be diminished since you already have something in common—you are there to work. If you are the disciplined actor seeking success and fulfillment, who views her work as service to others, then people will more likely view you in a positive light, and thus you set yourself up to earn the respect of your colleagues and create the potential to build solid, genuine relationships.

OFFICE MATES AND RELATIONSHIP BUILDING

Use your time wisely with your Office Mate to create plans, set goals, and report on your progress. Here are some tasks that are utilized in the relationship building process:

- Create a list of everyone you know in "the business."
- Determine a strategy and a timeline for contacting those people.
- Set up meetings.
- Send thank-you notes.
- Invite people to your events, showcases, and performances.
- Continually update your Industry Contact List as you meet more people.

When you meet with your Office Mate you can:

- Report on any meetings you've had with industry professionals.
- Discuss the ways in which you'll follow up or have already followed up.

- Determine a follow-up timeline.
- Brainstorm new relationship-building strategies.
- Set a timeline for implementing those strategies.

Ask your Office Mate to help you improve strategies for coping with the challenges of relationship building. Set concrete goals and deadlines that make you accountable. Share your successful strategies.

We hope that walking you through the steps with relationship building illustrates how this book can guide your process. See if you can do the same with other elements related to the Circle of Work: auditioning, rehearsing, goal setting, seeking work, and assessing your work. It can be gratifying to see these tasks in a new, invigorating light.

ASSESSING YOUR PROGRESS

Below is a rubric that presents criteria you can use to assess your effectiveness in implementing the strategies we've presented. Rate yourself on a 5-point scale—1 being the lowest rating and 5 being the highest. The continuum below spells out measures for success. You might fall between one of the three stated measures. We have deliberately made the lowest end of the scale exaggerated. These are rock-bottom attitudes that reflect resistance to the concepts behind *Minding the Edge*. The midpoint (number "3") reflects a willingness to implement the concept, but there is still need for growth and improvement. The highest end of the scale describes an ideal implementation and integration of the concepts.

Honestly evaluate where you fall on the continuum for each criteria. You may want to discuss your findings with your Office Mate.

You the Actor/You the Person

I can clearly articulate my personal fulfillment needs.

1		3		5
Not so much.		I have a general idea of what they are.		I have articulated my fulfillment needs and understand them in a way that I can identify and pursue them.

I continue to recognize daily situations where I experience one or more of my PFNs.

1		3		5
I forget to think about it.		I remember to do this on occasion and have some success in recognizing my PFNs.		I try to focus on my PFNs and create reminders that make me more aware.

Disciplined Thinking

I effectively deal with disappointment.

1		3		5
I get angry, worked up, and stew over disappointments for a long time.		Sometimes disappointment still gets the best of me, but I try to deal with it in a more effective way.		I allow myself to feel disappointed and then move on and focus on my goals.

I think positively about my talent/abilities/self-image.

1		3		5
I usually let my self-doubt get the worst of me and spiral into a state of anxiety and uncertainty.		Sometimes I dwell on my self-doubt, but try to catch myself and steer my thoughts in a more positive direction.		I recognize that there are times of self-doubt, but I seek positive strategies to deal with it, focus on the talents and abilities I do possess, and look for support from others.

I avoid joining in negative conversations.

1		3		5
I love to gossip.		I try, but sometimes I get sucked in.		I politely and appropriately refrain from jumping on the bandwagon, or I remove myself from negative conversations.

I avoid talking about others in a deprecating way.

1		3		5
I feel better when I diminish others.		Usually, but sometimes I can't help myself.		I talk about others the way I would like them to talk about me.

I avoid neg-a-tors when I encounter them and have appropriate strategies when I have to work with them.

1		3		5
They make me nervous, so I cave in and I try to be their best friend.		Usually, but sometimes I forget, especially when they are funny or I agree with them.		I treat them with respect but try to steer clear of them.

I accept valuable, constructive feedback from people whose opinion I respect.

1		3		5
As long as I agree with it.		Sometimes.		I am open and discerning when I listen to feedback and accept it in the spirit in which it was intended.

I deal appropriately with valuable feedback that comes in the form of blunt criticism.

1		3		5
I feel intimidated or I get in the other person's face and let him have it.		I try not to let it get to me but sometimes it shakes my confidence and creates self-doubt.		I consider the spirit in which it was intended. While it can be unsettling, I evaluate its validity.

Disciplined Action

I can clearly articulate my long-term and short-term goals.

1		3		5
I just want to act.		Somewhat. Some of them feel a little vague.		I have thoughtfully considered my goals in specific and concrete ways.

I have a strategy to reach my goals.

1		3		5
It will happen if it's supposed to happen.		Some of my goals don't have a clearly defined strategy.		I continue to refine and evaluate the specific strategies that will effectively help me reach my goals.

I take steps every day to achieve my goals.

1		3		5
Success will come my way. No need to work for it.		I try to remember but get distracted and sometimes forget.		I am disciplined in my actions and motivated to take steps to move my career forward.

I've identified habits that will help me become a more disciplined actor.

1		3		5
Habits are boring. I'm an artist.		I have identified one or two.		I know the disciplined habits I need to adopt that will lead me to success.

I have started developing those habits.

1		3		5
Not yet. Now is not the time.		Sometimes.		Yes. I determined manageable strategies that will lead to more disci-plined habits.

The 80-Year Plan

I set appropriate timelines for achieving my goals.

1		3		5
I am going to be famous by the time I'm twenty-five or else I've failed.		I understand the concept, but I'm still unrealistic in setting certain timelines.		I recognize the need to be flexible in developing and reaching my goals.

Your Career Is Part of a Service Industry

I look for ways in which my career is of service to others.

1		3		5
I want to be an actor, not a social worker.		Sometimes I do. When I remember.		I recognize that there are numerous ways in which the work I do can benefit others, and I focus on that.

I can identify specific actions and events where I am of service to others.

1		3		5
If I'm going to be a success, I need to devote my time to me.		Sometimes it's easy to see how my work as an actor is a service to others. Other times I don't really look.		I look for the instances both obvious and not so obvious to see my work as serving others. I feel good when I view it that way.

You at Work

I am aware of the positive qualities I bring to a work situation and I know that people enjoy working with me.

1		3		5
I either need to get everyone to love me or I don't care if they enjoy working with me or not.		I want to get along in a work situation, but if it's not happening, I'm not sure what to do.		I know the positive qualities I bring to my work and identify other qualities I would like to develop.

I respectfully engage with everyone I encounter in the work place.

1		3		5
Unless I don't like them.		Usually, but sometimes people can be difficult, which makes it more challenging.		I respect the people around me and recognize the importance of doing my part to create a positive work environment.

The Circle of Work

I utilize the Circle of Work as a means of organizing the stages of my many career endeavors.

1		3		5
There are too many steps in the Circle of Work.		Some elements work for me, but I have trouble thinking about seeking work when I am involved in a project.		I utilize the Circle of Work and recognize the need to be consistently engaged in each aspect of it.

I utilize the necessary tools to enhance my success in each stage of the Circle of Work.

1		3		5
I have a head-shot and a resume. Isn't that enough?		I have a list of tools and try to use them.		I understand how each step of the Circle of Work fits into the "big picture" and effectively apply the appropriate tools in each situation. The tools in my arsenal are up-to-date and always at the ready.

Making and Keeping Connections
I view networking in a positive, constructive light.

1		3		5
I'm too shy, lazy, and dis-interested, so I don't do it.		It's a neces-sary evil, and I try to do it but I'm not always successful.		I view net-working in a positive light and recog-nize each situ-ation as an opportunity to build new relationships.

I continually seek opportunities to connect with others in the industry.

1		3		5
Let them find me. I'm a diamond in the rough.		Sometimes, but I have problems getting motivated.		I evaluate situations and recognize opportunities to create new industry relationships.

Getting Work

I can clearly articulate my type, and I pursue work that matches that type.

1		3		5
I'll let my agent figure out who I am and how to sell me.		I try to understand my type and pursue appropriate roles, but it's challenging, and I haven't given it as much consideration as I could.		I know my type and present myself at auditions in a manner that appropriately reflects that understanding.

I identify potential work opportunities through research and relationship building.

1		3		5
I wait to hear about auditions from friends.		I have some regular sources that I use to find out about auditions, but I don't use them consistently.		I do my homework and explore many avenues to find acting work.

I develop strategies to effectively create opportunities.

1		3		5
I believe in fate, and if I'm supposed to have an opportunity, it will present itself.		Sometimes I do this, but it can get burdensome and overwhelming. That's when I give up.		I do this regularly and generate new ideas for work opportunities.

Freaking Out

I allow myself the feelings that come with freaking out, but I take action to move to a better place.

1		3		5
No, I just freak out.		Sometimes it's difficult to seek solutions when I'm in that state, but I try.		I recognize that I'm freaking out, identify the cause, and take appropriate action.

Create Your Own Team: Office Mates

I have identified an Office Mate. We have set up a system for working together.

1		3		5
I don't need one. I'll figure it out on my own.		I'm working on it.		My Office Mate and I are moving forward with our strategies.

I trust my Office Mate to be on my side—to be my cheerleader.

1		3		5
I don't want to help someone become more famous than me.		I'm still looking for an Office Mate.		Yes. I trust and respect my Office Mate.

I am on my Office Mate's side—I am his/her cheerleader.

1		3		5
That's not important. *I* am important.		Most of the time.		I recognize the importance of my role as cheerleader and consistently support my Office Mate.

I employ good listening skills when I am with my Office Mate.

1		3		5
What did you say?		I try to listen, but I often have to remind myself that I'm not doing as well as I'd hoped.		I realize the importance of listening and practice good listening skills.

My Office Mate and I continue to develop action steps that will lead us to achieving our short-term and long-term goals.

1		3		5
I work alone.		Sometimes we get side-tracked. We connect too infrequently.		My Office Mate and I are developing concrete action and accountability steps that will lead us to complete our goals.

Chapter 16

Our Final Thoughts

The Ball's in Your Court

We feel confident that adopting the *Minding the Edge* strategies and mind-set can empower you as an actor. As you apply these concepts, the road to success may be more satisfying. We've presented a framework upon which you can hang your strategies and the advice of other professionals. You may want to come back to this book throughout your career. Read it again with these "4 R's" in mind: *revisit, remind, reflect,* and *revise*. Be willing to *revisit* this book. You won't absorb every idea by reading it once. *Remind* yourself of the important concepts and strategies that worked in the past or are pertinent in the present. Examine how they apply. As you progress in your career, you will experience different challenges and opportunities. Your career goals and personal fulfillment needs may change. If you're minding the edge you will continually *reflect* on those challenges, opportunities, goals, and needs and *revise* the strategies, tools, and systems that pave your path to success and fulfillment.

There are some great resources out there that will provide you with the specific details about finding work, getting agents, choosing teachers, locating information, and staying on top of industry trends. To get you started, we've included a partial list in the appendix. But don't limit yourself to those sources alone. Explore on your own and discover what's available to you. Research a city before you move there. Get the ball rolling while you're in school. Learn how to make a demo and a voice-over reel and do it before you leave school. Involve yourself in student films, so when agents ask for your reel you can show them something concrete. Arm yourself with information and begin building relationships before you graduate. Apply the Circle of Work to your current situation so you can develop the disciplined habit of adopting and utilizing it as a business model.

Dispatches from the Field—Carl

A few years ago, I got an anxious phone call from a student in mid-August. She was a rising senior theatre major and was panicked about graduating the following May. She had heard that Chicago was a great theatre town and wanted to move there but had no idea what to do, how to find a job, or where to live. We met for coffee and she had a mini-meltdown. I proposed that she and I do an independent study that would lead to a business plan and strategy for life in Chicago. She jumped at the idea. I knew that she was an incredibly focused, driven student and that she'd follow through on her commitment. She researched the city's theatres, casting directors, agents, photographers, acting schools, neighborhoods, transportation system, and cost of living. She read some of the how-to books we list in the appendix and discovered online resources that would help her get work. She flew to Chicago over spring break and looked at apartments. She created a website, did a few student films, made a reel, and wrote cover letters. In effect, she started her career in Chicago nine months before she arrived there. As you can imagine, she moved there after graduation feeling prepared to meet the challenge while many of her peers were still trying to figure out a postgraduation plan. In late April of that same school year, she and I had coffee. I asked her if she was nervous about graduation. Her answer was so incredibly memorable. "I'm nervous about moving to a new city and starting my career as an actor, but I'm not scared. I feel ready and excited. I think it's normal to feel nervous about such a huge change, it's the unknown." Jen is a remarkable young woman, and I was not surprised by the wisdom of her insight. Within weeks of arriving in Chicago, she auditioned for classes at Second City (the famed improv comedy school) and was accepted. Within a year she was a working actor creating successful projects and being cast in local productions. Her story is an inspiration to many young actors starting their careers.

Our hope is that you, like Jen, will use your time in school to set the wheels in motion, create professional relationships, learn about "the business," research, and get one step ahead of the game. If you do, you've made a commitment to *minding the edge.*

ACTOR'S TOOLBOX CHECKLIST

The following checklist may help you get organized. As with the rubric in the previous chapter, we set it up on a 5-point continuum.

Audition Book

Unacceptable		Passable		Excellent
Don't keep one.		Recorded a few. Records incomplete.		Always record audition dates, directors, contact names, and important feedback as well as my own evaluation of the audition.

Database/Relationship Building

Unacceptable		Passable		Excellent
Seldom/never did it.		Kept some records of contacts. Occasionally followed up after meetings and auditions.		Kept organized records/ database of professional contacts. Followed up with all contacts. Sent thank-you notes.

Office Mate

Unacceptable		Passable		Excellent
Got in an argument and stopped working.		Met somewhat regularly and did some goal setting, strategizing, and brainstorming.		Met on a set schedule. Productively used time to set goals, strategize, brainstorm. Supported my office mate.

Myself as an Office Mate

Unacceptable		Passable		Excellent
It's all about me, silly.		Was nice to my Office Mate.		Devised strategies, listened, supported, and invested in my Office Mate's success.

Headshot

Unacceptable		Passable		Excellent
Will wait until I graduate.		Looked at a few photographers' websites and contacted them.		Did my research. Have a headshot or will have one soon.

Resume

Unacceptable		Passable		Excellent
Banged it out. Barely.		Looked at others' resumes. Wrote a draft of my resume.		Researched resumes. Wrote several drafts. Sought feedback on my resume before writing the final draft.

Cover Letter

Unacceptable		Passable		Excellent
It's on my list.		Wrote a draft.		Wrote a few versions for different situations. Got feedback and revised my letters.

Elevator Speech

Unacceptable		Passable		Excellent
Will think of one when I get on an elevator.		Have a few ideas I've put together but haven't practiced it out loud.		Wrote it out. Practiced it a few times with my Office Mate. Continue to revise and rethink and write multiple versions.

Goal/Strategy

Unacceptable		Passable		Excellent
Will get to that soon.		Have a few concrete goals. Have thought about a few strategies.		Articulated my goals (both long- and short-term). Created strategies for short-term goals and have shared them with my Office Mate. Initiated projects and potential work for myself.

Seeking Work

Unacceptable		Passable		Excellent
Waiting for an agent to do this for me.		Identified agents, casting directors, theatres, online resources, trade publications, etc.		Identified the sources, people, publications, etc., and have created a file and system for contacting, researching, and identifying potential sources of employment.

Research on the Web

Unacceptable		Passable		Excellent
Too many online distractions.		Visited a few websites where actors can post resumes and seek work.		Researched websites and submitted my resume when it's appropriate. Continually use the web as a means of seeking work opportunities.

My Website

Unacceptable		Passable		Excellent
A Facebook page is better than a website.		Looked at a few actors' websites and started work on one.		Launched a website with my headshot, resume, and reel.

Business Cards

Unacceptable		Passable		Excellent
Don't need a business card. Can use a napkin to write out my info.		Looked into it and will get them after graduation.		Ordered business cards with my cell and headshot printed on them.

Business Hours (Time Spent Developing My Business)

Unacceptable		Passable		Excellent
Will work on my career when the mood strikes.		Need to keep more frequent business hours to accomplish my goals.		Scheduled weekly times to work on my career and consistently adhere to my schedule.

Appendix

The following resources may be useful to you, and there are more out there.

BOOKS ABOUT THE BUSINESS

Acting As a Business: Strategies for Success. Brian O'Neil. Revised Updated Edition. New York: Vintage Books, 2009.

The Actor's Workbook: How to Become a Working Actor. Valorie Hubbard and Lea Brandenburg. Boston: Pearson Allyn & Bacon, 2009.

Ask an Agent: Everything Actors Need to Know About Agents. Margaret Emory. New York City: Backstage Books, 2005.

Audition. Michael Shurtleff. New York: Walker & Co, 1978.

Auditioning: An Actor-friendly Guide. Joanna Merlin. New York: Vintage Books, 2001.

The Business of Acting. Brad Lemack. San Marino, CA: Ingenuity Press USA, 2002.

How to Sell Yourself as an Actor. K. Callan. 6th Ed. Studio City, CA: Sweden Press, 2008.

A Practical Handbook for the Actor. Melissa Bruder, Lee Michael Cohn, Madeleine Olnek, Nathanial Pollack, Robert Previtio and Scott Zigler. New York: Vintage Books, 1986.

The Tao of Show Business: How to Pursue Your Dream Without Losing Your Mind. Dallas Travers. Dallastown, PA: Love Your Life Publishing, 2008.

What They Don't Teach You at Film School. Camille Landau and Tiare White. New York: Hyperion, 2000.

SELF-HELP AND POSITIVE THINKING BOOKS

The Artist's Way. Julia Cameron. 10th Ed. New York: J. P. Tarcher/Putnam, 2002.

Excuses Begone!: How to Change Lifelong, Self-Defeating Thinking Habits. Dr. Wayne Dyer. Carlsbad, CA: Hay House, 2009.

The Game of Life and How to Play It. Florence Scovel Shinn. Mineola, NY: Dover Publications, 2008.

How to Talk to Anyone: 92 Little Tricks for Big Success in Relationships. Leil Lowndes. Chicago, IL: Contemporary Books, 2003.

The Power of Positive Thinking. Dr. Norman Vincent Peale. New York: Fireside/Simon & Schuster, 2003.

Quiet Your Mind: An Easy-to-Use Guide to Ending Chronic Worry and Negative Thoughts and Living a Calmer Life. John Shelby. Novato, CA: New World Library, 2004.

Resurfacing: Techniques for Exploring Consciousness. Harry Palmer. Altamonte Springs, FL: Stars Edge International, 2002.

The 7 Habits of Highly Effective People. Stephen Covey. New York: Free Press, 2004.

Start Late, Finish Rich: A No-Fail Plan for Achieving Financial Freedom at Any Age. David Bach. New York: Random House, 2005.

10 Simple Solutions to Worry: How to Calm Your Mind, Relax Your Body & Reclaim Your Life. Kevin Gyoerkoe and Pamela Wiegartz. Oakland, CA: New Harbinger Publications, 2006.

The War of Art: Break Through the Blocks and Win Your Inner Creative Battles. Steven Pressfield. New York: Grand Center Publishing, 2003.

You Can Heal Your Life. Louise Hay. Santa Monica, CA: Hay House, 1984.

ONLINE RESOURCES

Auditions, Current Industry Information, and Research

Actorsaccess.com   audition information, self-submissions

Backstage.com   audition information, industry updates

Bluegobo.com   research materials—videos of musical numbers from televised Broadway shows dating back to the 1940s.

Broadwaystars.com   theatre updates, current productions

Broadwayworld.com   theatre updates, current productions

Deadline.com   industry updates (mostly film and television)

Hendersonenterprises.com   *Casting Directors Guide*

IMDB.com/IMDbPro.com   entertainment data, representation listings, company and employee contact details.

Jackplotnick.com   audition insights

Playbill.com   theatre updates, current productions

Theatredirectories.com   listings of summer and regional theatres, training programs

Theatricalindex.com   current theatre information

Truonline.org (Theatre Resources Unlimited)   membership required, theatre information

Variety.com   industry information

NOTES

NOTES

NOTES

NOTES

NOTES

NOTES